Journey to You

Fierce Freedom, Authentic Passion

Gracious God

Diana Asaad

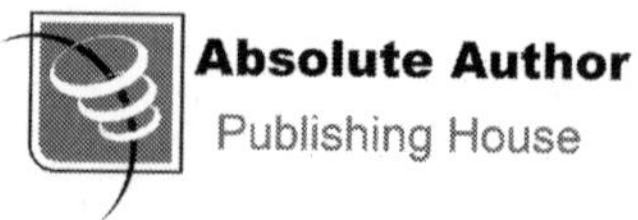

Journey to You

Scripture taken from a variety of sources and are listed in the Reference Section in the back of the book.

Interior Designer: Dr. Melissa Caudle

Relentless Publications
in collaboration with Absolute Author Publishing House (AAPH)
ISBN-13: 978-0-9983999-3-5

Library of Congress Cataloging in Publication Data

Asaad, Diana/Journey to You

p. cm.

1. Memoir 2. Religion 3. Spiritual

DEDICATION

For my sisters near and far, may these stories draw you closer and spark in your heart an eternal flame.

For the worshippers longing to be free, may you live in relationship with the Lover of your soul like never before.

To my sweet husband and friend, Hany, your love points me to a greater love, and that is all I could have dreamed of. Thank you. To Lily, Grace, and Hannah, my greatest blessings, may you know Jesus as vibrantly as Mary of Bethany.

Love,

Diana

CONTENTS

Introduction

Many women yearn for a deeper relationship with God: a more meaningful, intimate exchange that overflows into all other areas of their lives. These pages provide a practical plan to fill the void that echoes deep inside and lights a path of journey to greater meaning.

Spiritually minded women often find themselves trapped in cycles of defeat. I hope to offer you help if you are feeling disconnected and discouraged by uncovering secrets hidden in the story of Mary of Bethany. As we journey together through this book, I hope to provide you with a practical plan to get unstuck and develop a deeper relationship with Jesus by learning to apply Mary's secrets. I want to help guide you to freedom from fear and apathy into fierce faith and authentic passion, which is found at the feet of a gracious God.

Holiness is so unattainable in our minds. It is a standard that seems impossible to achieve. But when we understand the meaning of holiness and our true calling as Christians, we understand God's heart for us a bit better. The opposite of holy is not unholy, but common. Holy literally means to be set apart. Different. That is what God is calling for His people: to be set apart from all others. To be "Divinely Different". To stand out from the crowd. To have and be something that stands out from the common. Separated from the world. Though we are in the world, we are not of this world.

The Biblical story of Mary from Bethany has consumed my life. The applicable treasure hidden throughout the story has completely unraveled my thinking, delivering me from limiting beliefs and fear. I pray that it does the same for you.

Actions speak louder than words. Mary of Bethany embodies that saying. Our time together is focused on a woman who was recorded in the Bible as speaking one sentence. But her reach surpasses generations. Mary of Bethany loved God first and with everything she had.

Mary's story provides a framework for us to live an intimate, victorious, beautiful life connected to our creator. In Luke 10, we see Mary's thoughts. In John 11, we see her feelings. In John 12, we see her actions, and Jesus says, she has done a beautiful thing to me. She did what she could. When Mary sat at Jesus feet and heard His word she recognized Him as the *Prophet*; when she fell at Jesus feet in grief she knew Him to be the sympathizing *High Priest*; as she anointed His feet and head she knew Him to be the *Lord* and *King* in whose hands could be found the keys of death and the grave. Had Jesus not prevailed over death and raised her cherished brother? My heart's desire is to do a beautiful thing for Jesus as Mary did – that we all do something beautiful for Jesus. Do what we can: pray, build, give, listen, bless, and love.

All four gospels include a scene with a woman anointing Jesus, but the details vary quite a bit. Differences include when the event took place, which woman did the anointing, and whether it was Jesus' head or feet that she anointed. Scholars attribute the differences partly to the particular meanings that each gospel writer wanted to convey, because each gospel has its own distinctive emphasis, its own way of making meaning of Jesus's life. But I have to say that John's version of the story is to me the most irrational of them all – and – I would argue, maybe for that reason, the most beautiful.

Anointing someone's head with oil could have made sense. Anointing the head of a dinner guest was a familiar gesture of hospitality in that ancient culture. So if Mary had anointed Jesus's head with oil, her act would have been somewhat customary, a gracious and familiar expression of welcoming a guest. What's more, anointing his head would have recalled how in Old Testament times a prophet anointed the head of the Jewish king (2 Kings 9:1-13, 1 Samuel 10:1). Anointing Jesus's head would have meant that she recognized Him as the Messiah – literally, the anointed one. But the rest of the story provides more profound implications.

As we journey together through these pages, you will discover:

- You can change how you see yourself. Our past does not dictate our future.
- Jesus invites us deeper into relationship with Him.

- God will unfold His best plans in your life if you allow Him to.
- Anointing Jesus's head and feet was customary and has meaning for us today.
- Pride sneaks into our lives but we have been given tools to overcome it.
- Jesus had a scent that we can carry everywhere we go.
- The best defense for those who don't understand your heart and your worship is sincerity.
- Look at people with eyes of compassion and see them differently.
- Appreciate the secret of death and resurrection that Mary was one of the few to understand ahead of time.
- How to collect time, money, and resources for a purpose that matters.

Each chapter ends with the following format:

***Dig Deeper Devotion**:* Provides information to deepen our understanding

Meditate on these verses: Offers scriptures for you to reflect on and hide in your heart

***Challenge**:* Presents an opportunity to apply the teaching points from the chapter to your life today

Connect: Gives you a place to write back to God about your life, what you read, or a request on your heart

Prayer: Shares a quick prayer to help guide you and develop these principles.

God seems to take a peculiar delight in showing His love to the heart that wholly chooses Him. So choosing Him must be a single choice. Christ describes it in the words, "One thing is needful." Paul says, "This one thing I do." If there is one thing needful, then all other things are not needful. Unnecessary, non-critical, earthly things can come or go, can be for us or against us, yet all the time our soul can enjoy uninterrupted love and the presence of Christ. We are amazingly lifted above the force and influence of the distractions. Let's align our lives to God's purposes and watch what unfolds. I promise it will completely blow your mind.

I'm so excited to journey with you!

Diana

The scripture references in their entirety are:

John 12:1-8, *"1 Then, six days before the
Passover, Jesus came to Bethany, where Lazarus
was who had been dead, whom He had raised from
the dead. 2 There they made Him a supper; and
Martha served, but Lazarus was one of those who
sat at the table with Him. 3 Then Mary took a
pound of very costly oil of spikenard, anointed the
feet of Jesus, and wiped His feet with her hair. And
the house was filled with the fragrance of the oil.
4 But one of His disciples, Judas Iscariot, Simon's*

son, who would betray Him, said, 5 “Why was this fragrant oil not sold for three hundred denarii and given to the poor?” 6 This he said, not that he cared for the poor, but because he was a thief, and had the money box; and he used to take what was put in it. 7 But Jesus said, “Let her alone; she has kept this for the day of My burial. 8 For the poor you have with you always, but Me you do not have always.” (NKJV)

Matthew 26:6-13, *“6 Meanwhile, Jesus was in Bethany at the home of Simon, a man who had previously had leprosy. 7 While he was eating, a woman came in with a beautiful alabaster jar of expensive perfume and poured it over his head. 8 The disciples were indignant when they saw this. “What a waste!” they said. 9 “It could have been sold for a high price and the money given to the poor.” 10 But Jesus, aware of this, replied, “Why criticize this woman for doing such a good thing to me? 11 You will always have the poor among you, but you will not always have me. 12 She has poured this perfume on me to prepare my body for burial. 13 I tell you the truth, wherever the Good News is preached throughout the world, this woman’s deed will be remembered and discussed.”* (NLT)

Mark 14:3-9, *“While he was in Bethany, reclining at the table in the home of Simon the Leper, a woman came with an alabaster jar of very expensive perfume, made of pure nard. She broke the jar and poured the perfume on his head. 4 Some* *of those present were saying indignantly to one another, "Why this waste of perfume? 5 It could have been sold for more than a year's wages and the money given to the poor." And they rebuked her harshly. 6 "Leave her alone," said Jesus. "Why are you bothering her? She has done a beautiful thing to me. 7 The poor you will always have with you, and you can help them any time you want. But you will not always have me. 8 She did what she could. She poured perfume on my body beforehand to prepare for my burial. 9 Truly I tell you, wherever the gospel is preached throughout the world, what she has done will also be told, in memory of her."* (NIV)

Luke 10:42, *"There is only one thing worth being concerned about. Mary has discovered it and it will not be taken from her."* (NLT)

Part One

Fierce Freedom – Scandalous Worship

Chapter 1: What's in A Name?

> *"Now a certain man was sick, Lazarus of* ***Bethany, the town of Mary*** *and her sister Martha.* [2] *It was* **that Mary** *who anointed the Lord with fragrant oil and wiped His feet with her hair, whose brother Lazarus was sick."* – John 11:1-2 (NKJV)

I was born into this world and given the name Diane Abraham Bisheit. Not many people know that was my name because "name confusion" was just a part of my upbringing. At about six years old, I came home crying to my parents that the kids were making fun of my last name. I was bullied and called other things that sound similar but smell terribly worse. Not fully understanding their taunting and only wanting the stinky poop name-calling to stop, my parents resolved the issue very diplomatically… they moved us thirty miles away and changed our last name to Nazear, my father's father's name.

I wish I could say the "name confusion" ended then, but no such luck. It was in the sixth-grade promotion ceremony that a new can of worms was opened. I had to be called by my full name. And the culture we come from doesn't have bias as to whether you are born male or female, your middle name was your father's first name, regardless. How embarrassing! All of my perfect classmates with their perfect names were called, one at a time, Kathy Nicole Jones, Karen Ann Lee,... and then... Diana Abraham Nazear, followed by an uproar of laughter and sneers and a forced *shhh* from the principal. If I had a shell to crawl into, I would have gladly.

At sixteen, I once again faced head on "name confusion." I had worked hard throughout my high school years and was preparing for my SAT test, so naturally, we had to bring in our birth certificates as identification at that time. When I got mine from my parents a sense of awe washed over me as I held it for the first time in my own hands. Then upon further inspection, I realized that it said Diane on it. WHAT?! For sixteen years I was Diana! No big deal, right? Wrong! Anyone with a name like Christine will tell you they are not Christina! Shaking my head, I confronted my parents as to why they raised me with a name that was not my birth name. To which they replied, "Oh, we couldn't spell it, so we asked the nurse too. It's not a big deal." I boiled inside and secretly despised my immigrant parents' lack of spelling skills. I learned to justify my name every time I officially had to. "My name is legally Diane, but I go by Diana; it's my parent's fault," was my memorized line.

There were a few other times that "name confusion" reared its ugly head, (one involved an internal name change that still has some family members calling me Becky...don't ask). The last and final time I faced "name confusion", was when I looked up the meaning of my name. I had been sensing an underlying unhappiness with the roller coaster ride of identification, when I decided to dig into the meaning behind it. I had known early in life that my name was the Roman equivalent of the Greek goddess, Artemis, the goddess of the hunt, and felt such a disheartening once again. I had hoped for mountain-moving meaning, and I felt short changed. But it wasn't until many years later and some self-reflection that I felt compelled to dig further. I was challenged to find the essence of what my name meant and what I found rang true. Diana, divine, set apart. Well, I'll take that. I always wanted to feel that my name had more significance and so I clung to being Diana, the set apart, close to God one.

Mary's Name Confusion

Mary of Bethany had some "name confusion" of her own. Mary of Bethany was her full given name; the implications, however, have deep meaning that alludes to a life where not much came easily for her. Mary literally means bitter. Her place, Bethany, was one of struggle. In the original, *bet* is indicative of house of. So Bethany can be broken down into *bet* – house of, and *any* – which in Aramaic means to struggle or to suffer. Wow. We see a woman whose name could have easily defined her.

Her name means bitter; her place was one of struggle.

Her background is a shadow and also a clue that no matter what kind of suffering or struggle we come from we can move forward into our destiny. So my question to you today is what is coming from your suffering or your struggle? What's coming out of your struggle? We can either claim beauty or bitterness. The choice is ours. Will we hold onto the names we have or redefine ourselves as Jesus sees us?

We see some of her struggle when her brother Lazarus dies. Jesus waited to come to Bethany. Mary and Martha had to learn to wait and believe that God is good amidst hard circumstances, loss, sorrow, even pain. Times like this are when our faith is tested and becomes gold. What we come to know of God, and the territory He inhabits in our hearts through the trials we endure, leads people to say, in hindsight, "I wouldn't have changed a thing."

There have been many times God didn't answer our prayers in the way or timing we wanted, but in the end it's far better. Even if the "far better", is our coming to depend on Him more deeply to prevail.

Gold is Being Forged

Philip Yancy says, "Faith believes ahead of time what can only be seen by looking back." One day you will look back and understand.

Lazarus had been dead for four days when Jesus came. Martha ran out to meet Him. Mary was real. She was in the house, overcome with grief. Until *He* called for her. She ran, fell at His feet, worshipped, and wept.

In John 11:33, Jesus was deeply moved by the tears of one who loved Him. And He is moved by ours as well. We know what happens next; Lazarus is raised from death. And Mary's story could have stopped there, but it continues on.

Mary did not have to choose the difficult path for her life that she did. She could have stayed in her struggle and in her suffering and wallowed there. But if she had, we would've missed important lessons that we can use in our lives today.

Maybe your name has always let you down. Maybe, it wasn't your actual name, but something you were called or some label – self or other imposed.

Jesus invites you to choose a new path; a new name. In the book of Revelation 2:17, it says, "Are your ears awake? Listen. Listen to the Wind Words, … I'll also give a clear, smooth stone inscribed with your new name, your secret new name." (MSG) Jesus sees you differently and He has a perfect, secret new name for you. He longs for you to start to see yourself as He sees you. Abundant. Beautiful. Blessed. Enough. Loved. It's a smorgasbord of goodness, help yourself.

Dig Deeper Devotion

Are you in a place of bitter struggle? Mary unlocked secrets to breaking free from that cycle and gaining an intimacy with God not many people discover.

What labels can you start to peel off of yourself and bring to Jesus?

Meditate on These Verses

> Revelation 2:17, "Are your ears awake? Listen. Listen to the Wind Words, … I'll also give a clear, smooth stone inscribed with your new name, your secret new name."(MSG)
>
> Isaiah 43:1, "But now, O Jacob, listen to the LORD who created you. O Israel, the one who formed you says, "Do not be afraid, for I have ransomed you. I have called you by name; you are mine."

Challenge

Look up your name. Search for meaning that you didn't know before. Ask God how He sees you and what He calls you.

____

____

____

____

____

Connect

Write back to God about your life, what you read, or requested on your heart.

____

____

____

____

____

____

____

____

Prayer

Dear Lord, help us develop our identity in You. May we see ourselves how You see us and hear what you call us. Amen.

Chapter 2: Linger, Bask, Soak

The ONE Thing

*"There is **only one thing worth being concerned about**. Mary has discovered it, and it will not be taken away from her."* – Luke 10:42 (NLT)

Busy. It is a four-letter word. I like to be busy. Just ask my friends and family. If I don't have twelve projects going on, I'm just not happy. Years ago, I decided that having two children, a husband, a business, a ministry and half a dozen hobbies was not enough, so I decided to enroll in college again and complete my degree. That first day back at school was unusually crowded with multiple obligations, but the excitement of starting something new was a high all its own. So I ran around not leaving any room in my schedule for anything unexpected, and low and behold a hiccup came. Something else demanded my attention and now I was running late. That couldn't happen on the first day! I rushed around like a chicken with her head cut off, grabbed my stuff, threw my kids at my husband and raced to school. It wasn't until I was walking to the classroom that I took my first breath to calm myself and looked down at my feet. There, staring back at me, were two of the same shoes, just one black and one white! Really?! Way to make an impression, Diana. So when we went around introducing ourselves, I took it as an opportunity to laugh at myself because, with the exception of going barefoot, there was no escaping ridicule, or at least a few sideways glances.

Dangerous Distractions

Distraction is a funny thing. It can be well intentioned, but truly consuming. Distraction can derail the best-laid plans for success. Then when we come up for air, we are often disoriented asking, "How did we get here?"

Surely, you've been distracted a time or two. Ever get somewhere and not remember driving there? Ever think you left the stove on? Distractions come with a hefty price tag. **Distractions devour destiny.**

Catch Composure

Have you ever met an individual that just seemed to have God's presence all over them? It seemed that they possessed a walk with the Lord that was head and shoulders above anything you have ever experienced yourself, and you wondered how they accomplished it. I think the answer lies in what they have discovered.

Some people have learned to abide at the feet of Jesus as they go through life and this translates into peace of heart, power of life and purpose before God.

I think many of us long for this type of connection. Maybe you feel this way? To be constantly and consistently filled with the Spirit of God and to be found at the feet of Jesus is something worth seeking.

The Bible states it this way in John 15:4-5, "Abide in Me, and I in you. As the branch cannot bear fruit of itself unless it abides in the vine, so neither can you unless you abide in Me. I am the vine, you are the branches; he who abides in Me and I in him, he bears much fruit, for apart from Me you can do nothing." (NASB)

I remember when God was whispering that word "abide" to my heart. It was something I dreaded, like a child in punishment who can't yet see that it's for their own good. I would awaken every day and ask God, "Am I done with abiding yet?" Only to be met with deafening silence. I knew it meant there was more work to be done in my heart. I knew the quiet moments that tended to first unravel and unsettle me were meant to be pushed through. To hear what the Lord was trying to teach me through.

The Gospels mention a woman named Mary. She was the sister of Lazarus and Martha, and she is mentioned multiple times in the Gospel account. Most times Mary is mentioned, she is found at the feet of Jesus. Her experiences there can teach us all some valuable lessons about our own walk with the Lord.

Mary of Bethany was probably best known as Martha's sister. The contrast of the two parallels what is going on in our society today. We have busy hearts, yet we are all offered a better portion. Martha represents a busy and distracted church. She exchanged relationship with Jesus for service to Him. Martha was distracted with serving. It's not the service part that is the issue, it's the distracted part. What are you distracted with? Social media, commitments, thoughts? Whatever is your distraction, Jesus calls you to greater intention today.

The book of Luke the 10th chapter tells the brief story of these two sisters. "**38** As Jesus and the disciples continued on their way to Jerusalem, they came to a certain village where a woman named Martha welcomed him into her home. **39** Her sister, Mary, sat at the Lord's feet, listening to what he taught. **40** But Martha was distracted by the big dinner she was preparing. She came to Jesus and said, "Lord, doesn't it seem unfair to you that my sister just sits here while I do all the work? Tell her to come and help me." **41** But the Lord said to her, "My dear Martha, you are worried and upset over all these details! **42** There is only one thing worth being concerned about. Mary has discovered it, and it will not be taken away from her." (NLT)

Looking in on this scene at Martha's home, we can tell what each sister's priorities were. Martha was concerned with preparing the meal and serving her guests. Mary, however, was more concerned with being in the presence of Jesus. Being overly busy in His work, to the point where we have no time to spend at His feet, is not His best plan for us.

Martha opened her home to Jesus and did her best

to be a good hostess. Mary, on the other hand, opened her heart to Jesus and tried her best to love the Lord. Too often, we are more like Martha than like Mary. In our zeal to serve the Lord, we wind up ignoring Him! While Martha labored, Mary listened. She found a place of stillness at the feet of Jesus.

The more time we spend at His feet, the easier it is to make time with Jesus a priority in life. The greater He gets in our eyes, the smaller other things seem to become. Ask yourself this question: Is sitting at Jesus's feet a priority in my life? We need to seek this place of stillness before the Lord!

Sit at Jesus's feet. Jesus woos us and invites us deeper. Jesus desires an intimate relationship with us. Come to His feet and ask Him to talk to you. I promise, hearing a Word from the Lord whispered to your heart can make all the difference in the world. Be relentless. Don't go until you hear from Him. It's worth it, and He always honors a seeker's humble heart.

Mary didn't hear preaching about Jesus, she heard *from* Him. She wasn't satisfied hearing of or about Him. Be like Mary – intentional, press in, and don't let this day pass without a message from Him.

The Good Portion

Jesus called sitting at His feet the good portion. The good portion, is the ONE Thing. A living, breathing, relationship with Jesus is what He seeks of us, and that is the ONE thing that will not be taken from us. Learn from Him, listen to Him, lean into His words.

Mary chose the good part. "But one thing is needed,

and Mary has chosen that good part *(or portion)*, which will not be taken away from her." Luke 10:42 (NKJV). Here you have the key to Mary's marvelous life. She chose the more excellent way. The word "chosen" in the above quotation explains the difference between the two sisters in Bethany. Some would try to make it appear that the difference between Mary and Martha was a purely natural one – a mere question of temperament. No – it is about a choice.

The same choice is set before us daily. Will we seek Jesus first or forsake Him for our own agenda?

Linger My Child

My youngest child likes to linger. She just likes to be around her momma. Don't think for a moment that I take her for granted. I have two older children. But for now, I will bask in the dawdled mornings laced with kisses and the last baby breaths I can muster.

I know what it is to linger, and I know how to live a rushed life. When I take the time to connect upwardly first, sitting at Jesus' feet, I see my day take a different path. I am just not as nice to those closest to me when I don't intentionally take the time out to savor in His presence. A luxury, some might call it, but in all reality, it is an absolute necessity if I want to carry out the will of God in my life. Isn't it amazing that the One who can do the most, the quickest is often the last One we turn to in a time of need?

Jesus says in Matthew 11:29, "Take my yoke upon you. **Let me teach you**, because I am humble and gentle at heart, and you will **find rest** for your souls."

How can He teach us if we never listen? Are we teachable? Are we willing to STOP and sit at His feet and let Him teach us? Tune out the noise of this world and tune in to what He is whispering to your heart.

When we as followers take the time to sit at Jesus' feet like we should, it makes a statement. We are telling the world that He is supreme in our lives. We are showing them that He is important to us and that we are not ashamed to be associated with Him. Sitting at Jesus feet will show on you! People will know when you spend time with Him. By the way, it will also show on you when you do not take the time to sit at His feet.

Sit at His Feet

More than anything else, Mary loved to sit quietly and peacefully at Christ's sacred feet and become lost in His revealing of the truth. Mary, more than any other individual in the New Testament, was associated with His feet, showcasing her humility, reverence, and hunger for spiritual knowledge. She sat at His feet as a disciple, eager to learn His will and Word, fell at His feet in worship and grief, anointed His feet with precious ointment and wiped His feet with her long hair—all of which is in keeping with her spiritual character.

Believing Jesus to be the prophet, she drank of the teachings He alone could impart as "the Truth."

What does Jesus long for? What does He want more than anything else from us? To love Him. With all our heart, soul, and mind. (Matt 22:37). The highest and most important thing we can do with our lives is to love

God. Only then can we reflect the heart of God to this world and love others.

When we love Jesus, it then becomes the fuel that fires every other good work in our lives. Oh, and loving Jesus, well that's just the heart's natural response to knowing Him. Spend a lot of time at Jesus' feet. At the feet of Jesus, we find a place of stillness and direction. So if you are seeking God's will for your life…befriend Him. Become His disciple.

She sat at His feet. What an image of contentment, peace, and humility. Reminds me of my lingering child when she crawls into my lap to just *be*.

I wonder if this is part of the process known as sanctification. Sanctification is a beautiful gift, which takes all worry and instability out of our heart and deposits a rest and peace, which cannot be described. A sense of unmistakable fullness is realized. Sanctification is a process in which we become more like Jesus. What better way to be more like Him, then to sit at His feet and *be*? There we find a sense of being inwardly healed.

She Heard His Words

She sat at His feet and basked in the deep meaning of His words. Jesus' words of comfort, of love, sweetness, and tenderness that drew Mary to worship extravagantly. She yearned to give the highest possible expression of her personal love for the Master. Her act at the banquet beautifully demonstrates those who reach the highest state of divine connection and whose love then becomes fearless.

There is special blessing pronounced on those who have ears to hear what the Spirit has to say. Listen to the prophet Isaiah, "Hear and your soul shall live." So cease your useless struggling; silence the noise of your self-will; get quiet; listen to Jesus – only let His words remain in your ears, seep down into your heart, and it will initiate restoration.

Perpetual Patterns

We do what we know. We do what we are accustomed to. Even in her time of trouble, Mary did what she was used to…she fell at his feet. In our time of pain; debating, or arguing with God (like Martha did), doesn't help. Falling at His feet helps. After the death of her beloved brother, Lazarus, Mary is once again found at His feet looking into His face for the help she needs. What she finds during this encounter can help us all when we face difficult times.

Dig Deeper Devotion

Where do you find yourself? Are you sitting at the feet of Jesus listening to Him, learning from Him and just loving Him? He is worthy of our total devotion. I challenge you to come to His feet. Let's find our place there and be all that Jesus wants us to be.

Focus on what's important. Do not get distracted! Ask yourself these questions:

Has Jesus captured your heart?

Has Jesus captured your attention?

Is sitting at Jesus's feet a priority in your life? Do you choose the ONE THING?

____

____

____

____

____

____

____

____

____

____

____

Meditate on These Verses

> Matthew 11:29, "Take my yoke upon you. Let me teach you, because I am humble and gentle at heart, and you will find rest for your souls."
>
> Matt 22:37, "Jesus replied, "'You must love the Lord your God with all your heart, all your soul, and all your mind."

Challenge

How do we become intimate in a relationship with Jesus amid the distractions of life? Be intentional about spending time with God. Seek Him daily. Shift your perspective and understand that it is really more for *your* benefit than for Him.

Connect

Write back to God about your life, what you read, or a request on your heart.

Prayer

Lord give us grace to sit at your feet and listen to your voice. May we seek you more every day.

Chapter 3: The Precious

"Mary therefore took a pound of ointment of pure spikenard, very ***precious****, and anointed the feet of Jesus, and wiped his feet with her hair: and the house was filled with the odor of the ointment."* – John 12:3 (ASV)

Do you remember the book (or movie), "The Lord of the Rings"? The most memorable character for me was Gollum, a creature distorted by his obsession with a piece of jewelry. He called the ring "precious". It controlled his actions with such power that he would do anything to keep it in his possession.

Bowing to False Idols

There are many times in our lives that we unknowingly do the same. We become distorted in our thinking and in our actions when we hold something so dear that we cannot give it to God sacrificially. It becomes so precious that we inadvertently worship it.

I have bowed my knee to false idols in my life unintentionally. Idols often creep into the landscape of our lives in the form of thoughts. Mine were no different. I struggled with my weight for most of my life. But others' criticizing comments are often the fertilizer that grows thoughts into idols. It was some "well-meaning" relative's criticism of me that alerted me to my growing girth. A bout of anorexia and bulimia seemed to vex the demons for a short time, but really the problem grew roots in my life and took over every thought and action until I was obsessed with my weight and quickly ballooned up the scale. You don't wake up one hundred pounds overweight. It is a process that devours every corner of your life.

The more I held onto this way of thinking, the stronger my chains became and the more weight I packed on, physically, emotionally and spiritually. And it wasn't until I sought God for help in this insurmountable issue that He revealed to my heart that every waking (and sometimes sleeping) moment was consumed with these thoughts. I had a very precious idol. Leaving no room in my conscious to worship the true Solution. When I began to submit my thoughts and allow God to lead my heart in worship to Him, things began to change. Had I held onto the precious self-image I was trying to attain; I believe I would have remained stuck.

Too Precious

Mary of Bethany had something precious as well – about a pound of pure spikenard oil. The oil that Mary used cost 300 denarii, which was one year's salary. If we bring that to today's standards that would be roughly between $35,000 - $45,000. Can you imagine lavishing such an amount on Jesus? Mary had been the recipient of priceless truth from the lips of Jesus. Now she was extravagantly unrestrained.

She was willing to give up this treasure because of her love for Jesus. Mary gave her best. She gave her all to the Lord she loved. When we give less than our most precious to Jesus, we have not really sacrificed at all. It is not until we give our "precious" that we are truly displaying our love for Him. When we shortchange Jesus with our time, our resources and our talents, we are not displaying our love for Him.

His desire is that He be given our all, as we learn in Romans 12:1-2. "And so, dear brothers and sisters, I plead with you to give your bodies to God because of all He has done for you. Let them be a living and holy sacrifice—the kind he will find acceptable. This is truly the way to worship him. [2] Don't copy the behavior and customs of this world, but let God transform you into a new person by changing the way you think. Then you will learn to know God's will for you, which is good and pleasing and perfect." (NLT).

Allow Him to change your mindset about giving to Him. Don't give because you *have* to; give because you *get* to. It's a beautiful privilege that God adores because "it" reflects His nature, as a generous father. Offer Him your precious time, resources, talents and thoughts and see what the God of multiplication can do with a willing contribution.

Precious is Inconvenient

Many people treat the Lord like this man who called his girlfriend and said, "Honey, I love you. I'd climb the highest mountain for you; I'd swim the deepest ocean for you; I'd fight a jungle of lions for you; and if it doesn't rain, I'll be over to see you tonight." This isn't real love! Genuine love knows no conditions. Love is freely given and asks nothing in return. Do you love Him in the way He deserves, in the best and highest way that you can?

Mary gave to Jesus something that was very costly. Give to Jesus what is expensive. Give him first place not leftovers. She did not pour *eau de toilette*, or cologne; she poured the most precious oil out on Him.

God's Dollar

A little boy was given one dollar to buy a treat, and another dollar to put in the offering plate at church. After church the boy's father asked, "Did you make sure to put the dollar in the offering?" The boy replied' "No Dad, God's dollar got lost," as he sipped his soda. His father asked him, "Why did you assume that God's dollar got lost and not yours?" The boy replied,

"Because God wouldn't want me to lose my dollar and not buy *my* soda."

Do we assume that God's time and money, is disposable first in our life? Does the time we set aside as "quiet time" become the first to be taken off the table when life screams for our attention?

Precious blood deserves something precious. Pure. Expensive. Costly.

Mary poured out all she had to Jesus in an extravagant offering of worship. She spent her time, her reputation, and her resources. She ministered to Jesus in a magnificent way. There was nothing Mary owned that she wouldn't spend on him.

Mary gave to the limit of her love and ointment. Will the Lord say of us when we see Him face to face—You have done what you could? Do we constantly anoint Him as the chosen of our hearts? Are His feet perfumed with our costliest gifts?

The world may count a life wholly consecrated to Him as a life wasted, but only the life abandoned to His authority is the one truly worth living.

Loss and Suffering

What kind of loss have you suffered? Have you, like Mary, lost a loved one long before you ever thought you would? Have you lost a marriage? Have you lost whatever passion you had? Have you lost some other cherished relationship? Have you lost your health or a job? Have you lost an opportunity that now, in hindsight, you wished you'd grabbed – the job you didn't take, the call you didn't make; the trip that you missed. Have you lost hope?

Like Mary, all of us have lost something or someone important to us. And for many of us, it's not just one loss. It's one loss, after another, after another. As the losses pile up, so do the questions: "Where was Jesus when I was suffering? Why didn't he intervene to keep me from losing what was precious to me? Was I a fool to give my heart to him? Does he really care about me?"

Suffering is devastating enough; but what may be even more devastating is the thought that perhaps Jesus, who did nothing to prevent the suffering, doesn't really care after all. God cares?

Mary's trauma teaches us that the ordeal is not the end of the story. Jesus does care. He sees, and He cried with her. Just like Mary's trauma was not the end of her story, your trauma is not the end of your story. The Author isn't finished yet.

Jesus has plans for your loss that you don't know about. He doesn't intervene the way you want Him to precisely because He loves you. He has a plan to enlarge your faith. If you could see it now, it wouldn't make sense. When you see it later, it will take your breath away.

Dig Deeper Devotion

What have we given power to in our lives and worshipped as our "precious"?

Is it too precious to be poured out? Our family? Our careers? Our reputation?

____

____

____

____

____

____

Meditate on These Verses

> Malachi 3:17, "'They shall be Mine,' says the LORD of hosts, 'On the day that I make them My jewels.'"

> Isaiah 43:4, "Since you are precious and honored in my sight, and because I love you, I will give people in exchange for you, nations in exchange for your life."

Challenge

Examine your life and see where you have held back from loving Jesus as you should. Is it out of fear? Hurt? Pain? Begin with small steps of giving God precious things and see how He responds in your life. Start with giving Him your precious time, resources, talents or thoughts. Get excited about how much better God is at handling those precious things of yours.

Connect

Write back to God about your life, what you read, or a request on your heart.

Prayer

Lord Jesus, help us to not have things in our lives more precious than you. Guide us deeper into true worship and help us to see you as the most precious. May we love you without regard to how others see us.

Chapter 4: Lambie's Gone Missing

"Lord, ***if you had been here****, my brother would not have died."* - John 11:32(b)

A lamb. A stuffed animal. My youngest child, Hannah, has a strange attachment to a stuffed lamb. Lambie cannot really be called stuffed anymore; the stuffing has been loved out of that thing. Flatter than a pancake and now a shade of dismal gray no bleach can brighten, he is her ever companion.

Lambie is dear to my heart as well. You see, this special toy used to belong to my precious niece. Emily Joy graced us on earth for an all too short sixteen months and left a big void in our hearts when she went to Heaven. My precious sister gave each of her siblings one of Emily's toys as a comfort and a memory. Lambie was my lot and that's how he came into our family. The cute toy was tucked away in a box with too many emotions attached, until years later I was unexpectedly pregnant again. In setting up the nursery, he was gently put in a place of honor among the other toys. He was forgotten about once more, until sweet Hannah's eye caught him and grabbed the lamb never to let go, it seemed.

Nine years in and Lambie has joined our family on every adventure. He has traveled more than some people I know. He was Hannah's constant companion. One knew they were liked when she brought his dingy, limp form up to your face and "licked" you. That was Hannah's stamp of approval and my mortification.

As toys do, even the precious ones, Lambie got lost from time to time. My hubby, however, has Lambie "GPS" and could find him in no time. Each time he found Lambie, he would gently place him up above Hannah's mirror in her room so he could enjoy the moment of discovery when she spotted him. "Oh, silly Lambie" she'd proclaim and motion with sheer exhilaration for someone to bring him to her.

One time silly Lambie got really lost, and Daddy "GPS" must not have been working properly. Lambie seemingly disappeared into thin air after we had been traveling. After more than a few melt downs, Hannah fell asleep fitfully each night, praying that Lambie would come back to her. Each morning, she lifted her gaze above her mirror, certain Lambie would return to his usual spot after being lost. But no luck. We searched and searched, Lambie was nowhere to be found, and Hannah was heartbroken. We were all a bit heartbroken.

Best Laid Plans

Things don't always go Mary's way either. She blamed Jesus, when things didn't always go according to planned. Consider when Lazarus, her brother became sick and died. It didn't make sense; after all, her family was close to Jesus. Mary, Martha and Lazarus were experts in divine relationship. In fact, Jesus was their frequent guest. They were his friends. They knew He *could* heal. So why was her beloved brother dead?

No one likes delays. Whether it's waiting in line for an appointment or traffic. So why does God make us wait? We see others getting their answers, but when is our breakthrough coming?

Mary of Bethany felt disappointment as Hannah did, as we all do. The object of Mary's affection had disappointed her. She felt Jesus had let her down. Her security and her faith were challenged when Jesus didn't come through for her in the manner she expected. Her brother, and Jesus' close companion, Lazarus was sick, so the sisters sent word to Jesus. Jesus seemingly didn't answer and lingered where He was. Mary watched as things went from bad to worse in her brother's situation and all with no word from Jesus.

Sometimes Love Delays

John 11:5-6 tells us, [5]"Now Jesus loved Martha, and her sister and Lazarus. [6] *So*, when He heard that he was sick, He stayed two more days in the place He was." Did you notice the small two-letter word we often skip? SO. In other words, because Jesus loved them, he delayed! The reason for His delay, was because He loved them. In a way that we cannot fully understand, for their sakes, Jesus delayed. What a shift of perspective! So that they would have a greater revelation of Him than anybody else, *He delayed.*

Lazarus had been dead for four days when Jesus finally came. Martha ran out to meet Him, she loved Jesus as well. Mary was overwhelmed in a moment of heartfelt emotion. She was in the house, most likely overcome with grief. Until Jesus called for her. She ran, fell at His feet (her place of refuge), worshipped and wept. And Jesus shared her sorrow. (John 11)

Mary is only recorded in the Scriptures as saying one sentence. Her actions always spoke much louder for her than any words ever could. But her sentence reveals her deep anguish and conflict. John 11:32(b), "Lord, if you had been here, my brother would not have died."

She portrays a struggling dichotomy of faith and reality. I know you want what's best, so why haven't you come through for me God? Why, even though I had faith and waited on you, did you let me down? Maybe you have asked similar questions. And Jesus answers. Not always with words, but consistently with compassion. Jesus never corrects or reprimands Mary for her feelings. He simply weeps. Identifying with the pain of one He loves, yet knowing He is the solution all the same. He extends that same compassion to us today.

Pleading with God

Have you ever pleaded for something from God and got no reply? Maybe the thing you placed all your security in, your "Lambie," was snatched out from under you, and you had no idea what to do next. Jesus is not some aloof deity, disengaged and harsh. He wants to let you know that no matter your struggle, He feels for you and with you. And He has the solution. Better still, *He is the solution.*

Things don't always work out the way we envision them. Mary wanted her brother around and never imagined having to bury him. But God sees things differently than we do. He sees the end from the beginning and sometimes the struggle we are in is for a purpose we cannot yet comprehend. Take heart, sweet sister, He has your solution and we can trust His way is better for us, no matter the difficulties. Start looking at your situation with an eternal perspective and it becomes less of a struggle simply for the finality of it all. When we see how short our lives are and begin to live on earth with eternity in view, we start to see things as God does. He has us in His hand and He loves us so much that He is ever patient and forever kind, until one day we can see our circumstances from His perspective, even if that day is when we see Him face-to-face.

Not So Simple Surrender

Sometimes we have to simply surrender to the unfolding of God's plan. We could not make any sense at the time of my niece's passing. How could our loving God allow such a thing? But day-by-day He reveals His plan for our lives and what He turns to our good. Sometimes, we must stop asking, "God, where are you in all of this?" and begin to ask, "God, will you reveal yourself to me in this matter?"

Our life circumstances shape us and help make us into the people we are. Shared circumstances are the only access point into another person's struggle. How could I really help another person unless I have traveled down a similar road in life? My circumstances allow me access to another person's pain.

God has a better plan. He wants you to trust Him. And remember that He takes all and works it for our good if we love Him. Romans 8:28 says, "And we know that God causes everything to work together for the good of those who love God and are called according to his purpose for them."

And by the way, Lambie turned up eventually. He is still a valued member of our family. May Hannah's attachment to Lambie, help us to see our connection to Jesus.

Dig Deeper Devotion

Is there something that you struggle with that can be looked at with an eternal perspective? What delays are you experiencing? Can you begin to look for the opportunities in the deferments?

____

____

____

____

____

Meditate on These Verses

Romans 8:28, "And we know that God causes everything to work together for the good of those who love God and are called according to his purpose for them."

Isaiah 55:9, "For my thoughts are not your thoughts, neither are your ways my ways, declares the LORD. For as the heavens are higher than the earth, so are my ways higher than your ways and my thoughts than your thoughts."

Challenge

What circumstances have you been allowed to go through? Do you have unique perspective to offer someone who maybe traveling down a similar path in life? Can you offer comfort or support to those around you who are hurting?

Connect

Write back to God about your life, what you read, or a request on your heart.

____
____
____
____
____
____
____
____
____
____
____
____
____

Prayer

Jesus, we ask that you help us to see this life on earth with an eternal perspective. Help us to find you in the details and your peace in our difficult circumstances. Amen.

Part Two

Authentic Passion – Extravagant Love

Chapter 5: The Smitten Act Strangely

"There is only one thing worth being concerned about. Mary ***has discovered it****, and it will not be taken away from her."* – Luke 10:42 (NLT)

It was the kind of picturesque fall day that belonged on a postcard. My strict parents hustled to lead the clean-up crew that consisted of their four troops, spiffing up the house for guests. I couldn't be motivated that day, as my thoughts were directed seemingly at the vibrant foliage out the window. That's what I wanted them to think at least. Unbeknownst to them, my ponderings were much more focused. I was waiting to see *him*.

I remember the aroma as if it were yesterday. The heady scent of onion and thinly sliced steak still intoxicates and has the power to transport me back some thirty plus years. It was over cheesesteaks that my heart began to feel an unfamiliar sensation. My senses awakened, and my cheeks flushed every time he joked about the competition between us to make the best sandwich. I struggled to keep up with this boy's skill, though I'd never admit it. If there was one thing I knew, it was how to work my way around the kitchen, and no one was going to show me up. His quick wit and his knife skills rapidly won me over, and before long I was charmed.

Oh, the whimsy of being smitten. I was a tender fourteen years of age when I met my future husband. Although at the time, you couldn't convince me that this would be my betrothed. The first time we met all I could see was a hot-headed eighteen-year-old who thought way too much of himself. I think I was a little jealous of the attention he commanded as he played the keyboard for our church service. He really did think he was hot stuff. But through a series of events and a bit of meddling on my parents' part, there we were in the kitchen cooking together; and the stove wasn't the only thing heating up. It was in the kitchen that my heart started to warm toward him, and I was struck. Smitten. Oh, not just me, he was infatuated too and quickly showed me just how love-struck he was. Our affection began to sprout in that kitchen and soon I figured out just what happens when someone is smitten.

The following months contained a series of events that quickly captivated my heart even more. He had it bad. And being young and having many a fairy tale dream, I fell hard.

One time as I was leaving school, I was greeted with a note sticking out of my locker. Pleasantly surprised, I instantly knew it was from *him*. I read the note that led to a series of four more sappily sweet messages, and before long I found him waiting in the park on a swing holding flowers for me. He had driven more than an hour to see me for ten minutes and just let me know he was thinking of me.

I adored him and my actions showed it for sure. I bent rules, challenged boundaries, and pushed limits just to get to know him more and spend time with him. There were secret innocent rendezvouses where hands touched for the first time, and kisses were stolen, and faces blushed. What others said was right or proper didn't seem to account in this new world I found myself in.

I followed this enamored boy deeper and deeper into a forest of love. Uncharted territory for both of us, but terrain we could conquer as long as we were together.

Smitten is a funny thing. It's hardly logical and deeply emotional. Smitten gets up early and stays up late. Smitten breaks the rules. Smitten finds a way.

In the Bible we see a fantastic story of a love-struck woman, as well. Mary of Bethany was smitten. Jesus had captured her heart and her full attention.

In the book of Luke, chapter 10, we see Mary stakes her claim on some prime real estate at Jesus's feet. It was counter-cultural for sure, scandalous even, that this woman would claim that position. But she was smitten. She loved Jesus with holy adoration and expressed it through unabashed worship.

Smitten Mary; Serving Martha

Martha, Mary's sister, opened her home to Jesus and did her best to be a good hostess. Mary, on the other hand, opened her heart to Jesus. Too often, we are more like Martha than like Mary. In our zeal to serve, we ignore Him. While Martha labored, Mary listened. She found a place of stillness at the feet of Jesus. She found a place where her cares seemed to disappear. While Martha was distracted (verse 40), Mary was undaunted, calmly listening to the words of Jesus.

When we come into His presence, the burdens of life tend to grow amazingly light. It would do us good to learn to sit in His presence and forget about the cares of the world. If we learn to love the Lord more than our worries, we will be able to find that calm place in His centering presence. When our focus is on Him, other things tend to become strangely dim.

Unlike Martha, Mary was wholly present to Jesus, solely there for him. She stayed near to him, not wasting any of the brief moments He spent in their house. She simply sat at Jesus's feet and listened to Him. She didn't want to miss a single word He spoke. She had truly chosen the "good portion" (Luke 10:42).

In Bethany Jesus found open hearts that loved him and eagerly awaited him at all times. Mary laid all else aside; it was of secondary importance to her. She was completely captivated by Jesus. She had eyes and ears for Him alone, for Him whom her soul loved. To love Jesus, to hear words of eternal life from his lips meant everything to her.

Mary's vision was focused on Jesus as she sat at His feet. There, so close to him, she became understanding to what was on His heart. That happens to us as well, when we sit at His feet, we start to have a heart for what Jesus loves – the lost.

While Martha was worried over physical nourishment (verse 39); Mary was more concerned with getting her soul fed. In His presence, we will find food for our souls and strength for our journeys. Too often we find ourselves weak, lost, and lacking in spiritual vitality. Jesus invites us to come into His presence and nourish our spirits. Don't become spiritually starved, simply sit at His feet, and soak in His presence.

Often, the level of spiritual connection we are able to achieve in life is directly related to the time we are willing to spend in His presence. If everything in our lives takes precedence over being with Him, we become easily distracted and overwhelmed. The larger He gets in our eyes; the smaller other things seem to become.

Make Jesus your priority and find that your other obligations fall into place. Taking that small first step is all we have to do, then watch the response. Smitten happens in stages, but not calculated, formulaic ones. Rather, falling in love is like falling asleep, slowly at first, then engulfing every part of your being as you yield to its soothing appeal.

Extravagance Evokes Emotion

Something about what Mary did strongly speaks to our hearts even two thousand years later. It was an act of extravagant love — something one does when she only considers the object of her affection, and not the cost to herself. Or perhaps more specifically, after weighing the cost, finds it as being insignificant compared to the opportunity of blessing the Lord with a clear sign of affection.

Something about extravagant love evokes strong reactions in those who perceive it. It causes us to examine how much or how little we love, and we generally come up short in our own estimation.

All You Have Been Seeking

In sitting at Jesus' feet, Mary found fulfillment and contentment. What she discovered at His feet was worth more than anything in this world. In fact, in just sitting at the Lord's feet, Mary found something that millions live their entire lives and never discover. She found acceptance and real contentment. She found her true self. Herself as God created her to be.

Mary did not have to choose the difficult countercultural path that she did. She was likely ostracized and definitely spoken harshly to. How dare she, a woman, do as she did? She audaciously answered without saying a word. She simply sat. She lay her reputation on the line and deliberately placed her focus on the object of her love, Jesus. And she quickly understood that all other voices did not matter.

According to Hebrew tradition, the feet of a rabbi were reserved for the disciples of that teacher. In Acts 22:3, Paul says, literally, that he was educated "at the feet" of a rabbi. There is nothing unusual about this position. What is unusual is that the one seated at the feet of the rabbi is a woman. Rabbis had male disciples, and only men sat at their feet. What's happening here is a rabbi-disciple relationship, but a completely unconventional one.

We don't know what Jesus was saying, but we know that he didn't say this: "Mary, what are you doing at my feet? Don't you know this is where disciples sit, and that only men can be disciples of a rabbi? Go help your sister with the food." That's what Mary's sister, expected Jesus to say.

Martha, like everyone else except Jesus, thinks as the culture did, that a woman's place is in the kitchen and not at the feet of a rabbi. Jesus tells Martha that Mary has chosen, literally (some translations say), "the good part," the part of a disciple, and that he will not let anyone take that part away from her.

Mary crossed a cultural boundary by being intentional about where she sat. This was an all but outrageous practice in the day and age she lived. By sitting at the Master's feet, she declared, "I am your disciple. I will listen. I will follow!" She listened with undivided attention.

Disciples of the master would have been his friends. They would have been close enough to his life to know his thoughts and recognize his voice. So how do we know the will of God in our own lives? Befriend Him. Spend a lot of time at Jesus's feet.

If we seek God's will for our lives, we must draw closer to Him, become His friend. Only then will we discern His voice amongst all others shouting for our attention. We get to be friends with someone by spending time with them. Knowing them.

Extravagant Expressions

I wish I could say that my life was punctuated with acts of extravagant love for the One whom I love the most; but I cannot. I think there are things that I do that are clearly out of love for my Lord, but nothing that would say that I really put it all on the line. I hold back. Maybe you do, too. Why is that?

There are probably many reasons: we want to avoid embarrassment and criticism; we don't like to be in the spotlight; we worry about our futures and so hold things in reserve, just in case. God knows that about us, and He loves us anyway. But let us not be content living like we are living. Instead, let us always endeavor to become what we can be, as our ongoing expression of love for Him.

I don't know about you, but I'm not sure I've ever done nor ever will do anything of worldly significance. I sometimes wonder whether I've blown it — whether I've wasted my life, and I have nothing to show for it. But what this story keeps bringing home to me is that if Jesus takes note of my life — of the little things that I do for Him — then my life is significant after all, and in a way, I could never hope to achieve by being a superstar in this world.

Rocky Terrain

Life can be tricky at times. The roads we face can sometimes be uncharted and intimidating. No matter the terrain you are facing - loneliness, depression, rejection, stress, or confusion — follow Jesus deeper into His will for your life. Uncharted territory for you is ground you can conquer as long as you are together.

Mary chose the good portion (Luke 10:42), the better, more difficult, less-traveled path. Lord, give us grace to sit at your feet and listen to your voice. Lead us. Woo us deeper into your love. Be our heart's obsession. Take your rightful first place in our lives. Help us to see that in your love alone is our soul satisfied. May we be smitten with you.

Oh, and Jesus was pretty fond of Mary too… He's pretty fond of you also. While God's agape love is unconditional, and not based on feelings, it can never be earned. He simply loves, because He is love.

Dig Deeper Devotion

What is one way you can take a step toward loving Jesus? Is there something in your life hindering you from taking the next step of faith? Do you need to invite Him into your heart?

Allow God to come and take the controls of what is happening in your life. Only as we feed regularly on His Word will we stay fresh in our relationship with God. It is not enough to study the Bible—we must talk to God as we study. Bible study is meant to lead us to conversation with God by giving us the "conversational material" for our prayer life.

____

____

____

____

____

Meditate on These Verses

> 1 John 2:15-17, "Do not love the world or the things in the world. If anyone loves the world, the love of the Father is not in him. For all that is in the world—the desires of the flesh and the desires of the eyes and pride in possessions—is not from the Father but is from the world. And the world is passing away along with its desires, but whoever does the will of God abides forever." (ESV)

> 1 John 4:7-8, "Beloved, let us love one another, for love is from God, and whoever loves has been born of God and knows God. Anyone who does not love does not know God, because God is love." (ESV)

Challenge

Perhaps you too at one point in your life were drawn to Jesus and were touched deeply by his love for you. No one seemed to love you the way He did. He filled your life with faith, hope and love. Perhaps you have never experienced that.

Either way, He desires that we may know Him more, so be assured that the more we seek Him, the clearer His love becomes.

____

____

____

____

____

____

Connect

Write back to God about your life, what you read, or a request on your heart.

____

____

____

____

____

____

Prayer

Lord, give us grace to sit at your feet and listen to your voice. Lead us. Woo us deeper into your love. Become our heart's obsession. Take your rightful first place in our lives. Help us to see that in your love alone is our soul content. May we be smitten with you. *Amen.*

Chapter 6: Broken Jars

"While he was in Bethany, reclining at the table in the home of Simon the Leper, a woman came with an alabaster jar of very expensive perfume, made of pure nard. ***She broke the jar*** *and poured the perfume on his head."* – Mark 14:3 (NIV)

My dad had glasses issues. Really, he just had a sense of style that was all his own. His look was defined by the shiny, satin, silver shirts paired with a lavender flashy tie, under a grey suit, with its own sparkle. We didn't even try to figure him out. Glasses weren't just an accessory to him; they were a statement.

So, in the fourth grade, when I was told I would need glasses, naturally, Dad and his style stepped in.

Even at ten years old, I knew this would not end well for my social life. I gave Dad very specific guidelines for my glasses, of the "cool" thin, light blue-rimmed glasses that the popular kids were wearing and kept my fingers crossed. My well-intentioned father brought home the absolute opposite – only the best for his daughter. This ushered in two years of trying to break those repulsive large black thick-framed Ray Ban® glasses, that made my already large Egyptian nose look enormous.

Try as I may, those suckers seemed indestructible. I stepped on them, slept in them, and attempted to snap them. And with every small victory toward getting a replacement, my dad "fixed" (AKA duct taped) those hideous things. Then finally, I broke them beyond repair, and my heart sighed with relief. My fiasco was finished.

Mary broke something, as well. The jar that held the precious oil was broken.

Why did she break the jar and not just pour out the oil?

Mary broke the alabaster jar because she would not use it for anything else.

She made a complete sacrifice, and broke the jar.

Historically, an alabaster jar would have been a carved jar made of precious soft stone, which looks like marble, and would have been sealed. The most precious perfume or oil would be kept inside.

Mary didn't hold back. She wasn't going to save some of the perfume for later. She wanted every drop of perfume out of that bottle to give to Jesus. It was less than He deserved. And yet He received it. This jar could have been her life savings. This could have been her whole life.

According to some traditions, this was to be a marriage gift that she was supposed to give to her husband. It might have been an heirloom in the woman's family, and some historians say it might even have been kept as a dowry for her to pour out at her husband's feet before their consummation. In that sense, it would be a symbol of complete love, devotion, submission and obedience. This was her future. This was likely all she had, and yet she broke it open to give it all to Jesus.

That's trust. That's love. We should strive to show such love. Even giving our whole life, we acknowledge it is less than He deserves. And yet He receives it.

Are those things most precious to us sealed in jars as well? Our love and our families. Our hopes and dreams. All our plans. Our houses and possessions. Our gifts and talents; success and heartaches. Our ambitions. Our concerns. Our fears. Our needs.

One would probably think we are expected to pour out these things—our treasures—at the foot of the cross, and give them all to Jesus, just as the woman gave her oil to Him. But really, Jesus doesn't want our treasures. He wants more. All of us. Every part of our being.

So, we break the jar...

He wants us broken at his feet, like the jar. Only when we are fully broken, fully prepared to release all our treasures, hopes and fears, will God be able to say, *"Good, now I can begin a good work in you."*

When we are willing to be fully broken and accept Jesus into our lives, He begins to transform us through His Holy Spirit. It is a process of transformation, not a once and for all event, but it happens when we center our lives, daily and continuously on Jesus Christ, by reading His word, abiding in Him, understanding His character and in seeking more of Him and less of ourselves.

We don't need to fully understand it, just embrace it. It is a mystery as Paul says in Colossians 1:26, *"The mystery that has been kept hidden for ages and generations, but is now disclosed to the saints. To them God has chosen to make known among the Gentiles the glorious riches of this mystery, which is Christ in you, the hope of glory."*

When we embrace the life of Jesus in us, as we lay ourselves at his feet and say "Jesus, have all of me," we begin to see some of that glory. That is, we become more Christ-like. We do not have to strive for it, work harder at it, serve more for it. We have to focus on Jesus, and believe. To become mature in Jesus. Out of that transformation, He will use us everywhere we go and with everyone we meet and we will serve, not because He needs to use us or we have to, but because He is working in and through us. Jesus Christ working in and through you. Christ in you, the hope of glory.

I invite you to think of yourself as the alabaster jar. Are you willing to lay all of your broken pieces fully at the feet of Jesus? Are you going to continue to live your life your way, striving, working, serving and doing good things because that's the way you've always understood it was meant to be?

Some of you might be content with where you are in your relationship with Jesus. I am not. I want more, and so does Jesus. I challenge you to want more, too.

He wants all of us and He wants to work in and through us. It's a personal reflection and a personal challenge between you and Jesus. God's Word promises that if you lay down the broken pieces of yourself at the foot of His cross and give yourself to Jesus entirely, He will make you whole and you will find rest—true and complete rest. Then, you will have life to its fullest.

Profitable or Potential?

The alabaster jar of precious ointment of spikenard was profitable as it sat in that jar, but its ultimate potential was realized when it was poured out upon the head and feet of the Lord Jesus.

What was more precious to the Lord Jesus: the 'broken' alabaster jar of spikenard poured upon His head and feet – or she who bowed herself, broken, at His feet and anointed them with her tears and wiped them with the hair of her head?

Mary anointed the Lord for burial. Mary broke the alabaster jar. Was it not symbolic of her broken heart? A heart that was poured out before her Savior?

GOD is able to mend. Broken hearts. Broken homes. Broken hopes. Broken health. Broken happiness.

I'm **GLAD** that our Lord specializes in healing broken things! *He healeth the broken in heart, and bindeth up their wounds (Psalms 147:3 KJV).*

It's What's Inside that Counts

For years I identified on the surface with the infinite grace of God. How beautiful it was that Mary anointed Jesus. But I never comprehended the depth of the alabaster jar itself until I began to deal with many broken things in my life that I understood her alabaster jar and its significance.

In Mark 14:3-5, we see Mary break her alabaster jar and pour the contents of the fragrant oil on Jesus. We learn from Judas that the contents of the alabaster jar were worth more than a year's wages because it contained pure spikenard. We, like Mary, come to Jesus with all that we have of value, ourselves. He then abides in us and becomes the costly oil.

However, notice that in order for the precious oil to be released, the vessel **has** to be broken. There was no cap that screwed on, no top that sprayed a fine mist, no stopper that could be removed so the jar could be preserved in pristine condition. The maker of the jar designed it that way.

This is the way we are designed too. We are vessels made by the hand of the Almighty God for the specific purpose of allowing Jesus Christ to dwell in us. Through trials and tribulations, we are broken and what is inside (Christ), the precious oil, begins to come out. Troubles don't just come to followers of Christ.

They come to everyone. This is why we see famous people who appear to have it all – beauty, power, and money – seem to lose it when trials and difficulties come. Their vessels have no precious oil inside. So, what happens when there is brokenness? The content of their vessels pours out!

There is a place within each one of us that can be filled only by God. No matter how many things you buy, how much money you have, drugs you do, or partners you've been with, you will always be empty.

Reality television proves this point in spades. Shows filled with lives screaming for attention, searching for designer this-and-that, to fill an ever-growing hollowness. This is what our world has become: empty. How sad that our society defines itself by things that can be taken away in an instant, things that mean nothing when a tragedy occurs, things that can't comfort you when you are broken.

Now don't get me wrong, I'm not one who believes that you shouldn't have things. I'm one who knows things shouldn't have you! Things are just things.

So I ask you this day, what's in your vessel? Is it priceless and pure or is it filled with worthless things? I ask you to consider these things to encourage your spirit to action. Check yourself!

If you find that you have lost your focus, know that God is love and wants only to love not to condemn you. Fall back into His arms. They are open wide and waiting. If you have never felt the loving arms of Jesus Christ, know that He loves you so much that He suffered the cross for you. This day has been set before the forming of the earth as your day to be empty no more. Jesus has been waiting for you with arms open wide to welcome you to life everlasting.

Dig Deeper Devotion

God has emotions, and we were created like Him. How often do we hurt His feelings? When we just say words and don't fulfill our promises to God. Many times, we sacrifice something by words alone, and when the time comes to make good on our promise, we can take back the words so easily uttered. (Like Peter did when he denied Jesus)

Have you ever tried to break things that have a hold on you (like I tried to break my glasses)? Maybe you have dedicated things to God before, only to fall short on your promises. If God would only…then I will… (give me children…I will dedicate them to you.) Or you dedicate your resources or energy only to go back on what you've dedicated. Words without action equal a jar unbroken.

Stop reneging on the things that you have promised to God. Promised Him your time? Why is it the first thing on the chopping block?

____

____

____

____

____

____

____

Meditate on These Verses

Ephesians 5:2, "Live a life filled with love, following the example of Christ. He loved us and offered Himself as a sacrifice for us, a pleasing aroma to God."

2 Corinthians 2:14-15, "Now [God] uses us to spread the knowledge of Christ everywhere, like a sweet perfume. Our lives are a Christ-like fragrance rising up to God…"

Challenge

What areas of your life have you held back and not fully poured out to God? Why? Is it out of fear? Control? Lack of trust? Have you ever devoted something to God and then reneged on that promise? Offer your whole life and heart to Him today and let Him do a good work in you.

____

____

____

____

____

____

____

Connect

Write back to God about your life, what you read, or a request on your heart.

____

____

____

____

____

____

Prayer

Lord Jesus, fill me with your precious oil. Help me to live as a broken vessel, where you can be poured out through me to everyone around me. I surrender my heart and life to you today. Amen.

Chapter 7: King Over My Life

> *"And being in Bethany at the house of Simon the leper, as He sat at the table, a woman came having an alabaster flask of very costly oil of spikenard. Then she broke the flask and poured it on **His head.**"* – Mark 14:3 (NKJV)

I have always been a "Type-A" overachiever, which is just psychobabble to describe, in me at least, a pretty severe case of control freakery.

For as long as I can remember, my default approach to tackling life has been to work on projects and to deal with problems by myself. I'm the fixer. Where there is a problem or something not done, I jump in to get it done.

The difficulty with this is that every aspect of life cannot be controlled, and therefore I turned to the "god of food" for solutions. Is there anger in me? I can usually control that with a burger and fries. Am I resentful, irritated, overly ambitious, fearful? I can smother that with pizza. Am I depressed or bitter, suffering from a sense of life's unfairness? I can artificially perk myself up with some chocolate or cookies."

We do that at times – use food to deal with life.

As my weight ballooned upward, I began to own up to the truth that I had developed a complicated relationship with food. My predominant thought was, "I'll sort this out on my own." For years I tried all kinds of solitary solutions for self-mastery: personal improvement books, combative mantras, prayer and journaling, cleansing diets, intense exercise. You name it, I tried it. But to no avail. My idol became bigger and stronger.

I am, however, recovering quite nicely. How? I made a decision and decided to stick to it. I purposed to give up my false idols and surrender my control to the only One who really has control. God. I don't do it perfectly (not even close!) but I am much more aware of what I worship and how.

Mary Anointed His Head

When Mary anointed Jesus' head with the oil, it held great significance. In this deed she affirmed that He was the King of her life, for all to see. Kings in the Old Testament had oil poured on their head to represent that God's anointing was on them as the chosen one.

In the books of Matthew and Mark, Mary is shown anointing His head with the Spikenard from the alabaster jar. Mary anointed the *head* of Christ as He is the Head of all creation, the Sovereign God, and is worthy of all honor. She would do no less than have Him be King of her life. She signified her love for Him by anointing His head as the leader of her life, the king over everything.

In ancient times, Israel's priests and kings were ceremonially anointed with oil as a sign of official appointment to office and as a symbol of God's Spirit and power upon them. Moses anointed Aaron with oil to consecrate him as Israel's first high priest (Leviticus 8:12-13), and the prophet Elisha commanded his servant to anoint Captain Jehu with oil to seal him as king (2 Kings 9:3).

Consequently, when Mary anointed the Lord, it was a gesture of tremendous significance. Just before the cross, Jesus was being sealed as our King, Priest, and Sacrifice!

Make Him king over your life. Don't yield to your will or desire but let Jesus lead. God wants true followers and disciples. Jesus is asking, "*Do you really love me?*"

Many times, we want Jesus the Savior. Save me from... sin, poverty, sickness... but do we want Him as King? Jesus deserves all of me.

We bring Him our troubles. Problems tend to take precedence in our lives. My cares, my kids, my health... but He wants first place first. Mary knew He deserved first place.

Give the Keys to Jesus

Letting anyone else drive my vehicle is tough. I admit that at times I'm not the best passenger, especially when it's my vehicle. Do you "hit the brakes" on the passenger side when you think the driver's going to fast?

I think that anyone who's been driving a while secretly thinks they are the best driver around, especially when it comes to operating their own vehicles. I know it's true for me. I know how the car reacts to certain situations, the feel of the brakes, and the location of all the buttons. And I think that I can control that car better than anyone else.

So, when I hand the keys to someone else, I'm thinking things like, "Slow down before you get too close to the corner. Don't touch the radio!"

What's the bottom-line issue about letting someone else drive my car? The problem with letting someone else drive is that I have no control. And that's scary. It's my car, and I want control over it.

It's not a perfect analogy, but it's exactly why I struggled to let Jesus take the "wheel" of my life. I was afraid to give up control. I still am, at times.

But let me tell you that when I finally said to Jesus, "Lord – I'm tired of struggling in my own power to do this 'Christian' thing. I'm tired of falling on my face trying to live for you on my own. I'm tired of trying to make my own decisions about life. You take over," my life went in a whole new direction.

I found out that the Creator knew how to control the "car" of my life better than I did – because He created it in the first place, for His purposes.

Giving the keys to Jesus did not happen by default. It took an intentional, determined effort of my will. I had to tell Jesus that He's in control. It's not easy, and to be perfectly honest, there will be times when you wonder if it was the best thing to do. But it's the best thing we could ever do in terms of getting past the "lip-service" Christianity that most people live.

JESUS: King of My Life

Perhaps you are saying, *"I want Jesus to be king of my life. I want to do everything He commands of me."* Let me show you two of the wonderful blessings that come to all who enthrone Jesus as king of their lives.

Paul instructs us to come to Jesus, asking Him to give us dominion over all our sins and fears: "Do not let any part of your body become an instrument of evil to serve sin. Instead, give yourselves completely to God, for you were dead, but now you have new life. So use your whole body as an instrument to do what is right for the glory of God. Sin is no longer your master, for you no longer live under the requirements of the law. Instead, you live under the freedom of God's grace" (Romans 6:13-14 NLT).

God is saying, *"If you want to know abundant life—true, full life—then submit yourself to Me and I will give you life without fear, guilt or condemnation!"*

Second, those who submit to Christ's kingship will walk in peace—without fear or anxiety. "We have been rescued from our enemies so we can serve God without fear, in holiness and righteousness for as long as we live. Because of God's tender mercy, the morning light from heaven is about to break upon us, to give light to those who sit in darkness and in the shadow of death, and to guide us to the path of peace" (Luke 1:74-75, 78-79 NLT).

What a wonderful promise! If we will yield our lives to Him, He will shine His light into our darkness and guide us into peace and rest. You can tell when individuals have enthroned Christ in their heart. Their lives produce a peace that passes all understanding, and you can see that peace in the person's face and demeanor.

As we yield our control to Jesus, we find that Christianity becomes more than "lip-service". It becomes a daily, increasing reality in our lives.

Kings take care of us, but they also have the authority to command us. Can Christ command us? Or are we more typical of the modern person who doesn't like to be told what to do? Or perhaps we suffer from the milder form of this attitude that reduces and trivializes Jesus to being an "inoffensive hippie" who only says pleasant things about peace and flowers but would never rebuke us or command us to repent.

He is a compassionate King! But as His servants, we must come in line with His commands.

And so, again, the questions for us are: Is Jesus Christ your King? How will my life be different if Christ is King?

The conflict over who is king is acted out in our lives today. The world still wants us to worship all that is not God, and the culture rewards us when we do. But this conflict between the two Kingdoms, one of this world, one of the divine realm, becomes clearly delineated in the life of Christ.

Jesus tells us and shows us that the usual things people elevate as gods – power, wealth, food, celebrity and fame – are subjected in the Kingdom of God by the supreme values of service, love, and self-sacrifice.

Life in God's Kingdom is not about self-glorification, it's about surrender. It's not about big words, it's about powerful actions. Life in God's Kingdom is not about what the world values but what God values.

Author Barbara Brown Taylor tells a story about how when she was in seminary. She wanted God to tell her what she was supposed to do with herself. She prayed hard. Asked often, and the result, she said was this: God told her, "Do anything that pleases you – and belong to me." (An Altar in the World) Like Saint Augustine's similar spiritual instruction – Love God, and do what you will.

This could be read as a license to print money by a selfish person. Do anything that pleases you. Do what you will. Have a party. Knock yourself out. Except, pretty clearly, that's not what God said to – and through – Barbara Taylor and Saint Augustine.

The takeaway from these statements is absolutely not, "Believe in me, and act like a fool." Instead, the message is this: if you love God, if your values are God's values instead of the world's values, if Christ actually is King, then you will love as God loves, give as God gives, forgive as God forgives. If your values are God's values, you can't help but live as Christ taught.

Let Go and Let God

Monkey trappers in North Africa have a clever method for catching their prey. They fill a number of gourds with nuts and chain the gourds firmly to a tree. Each has a hole just large enough to allow an unsuspecting monkey to stick its hand inside the hollowed-out gourd. When the hungry animal discovers this hole and the treasure waiting inside, it quickly grabs a handful of nuts. However, the hole is too small for it to withdraw its bulging, clenched fist. And the monkey doesn't have enough sense to open up its hand and release the deceptive plunder in order to escape. So, it is easily taken captive.

The tendency to cling tenaciously to tempting treasure plagues unsuspecting humans and monkeys alike. The devil traps many Christians by appealing to their natural greed and carnal appetites, which leads to their spiritual downfall. As long as people hold onto worldly bait, they cannot escape Satan's trap.

Mary of Bethany is a great example of letting go. She let go of many things the world esteems as treasure, in order to anoint Jesus King over her life. Her fame doesn't come from the coveted traits the world typically associates with greatness. Mary occupied a special place among the followers of Jesus because she demonstrated three traits worthy of merit: a great love, a tenacious loyalty, and faultless devotion.

In order to "let God" do something in our lives, we first must "let go" of everything and everyone else! In the posture of surrendered control, we find freedom in His kingship over us.

In his famous speech, the Rev. Martin Luther King Jr. told how he would like to be remembered, and in doing so, he zeroed in on that ultimate question: If Christ is King, what does that mean? If Christ is ruler over our lives, Dr. King told them, then my Nobel Peace Prize is less important than my trying to feed the hungry. If Christ is King, then my invitations to the White House are less important than that I visited those in prison. If Christ is Lord, then my being *TIME* magazine's "Man of the Year" is less important than that I tried to love extravagantly, dangerously, with all my being.

How are things going to work out in our lives? I don't know, and neither do you. But we do know the shape of the story a loving God is writing: If Christ is King, we know Jesus waits at the end of that story, that He will see us, and know us, and that if we have done what He taught us, He will claim us as His own.

And, I have to say, that is question and answer enough for me.

Dig Deeper Devotion

Are you a control freak in some areas – with your kids, your spouse, or your home, at work, with your extended family? Are you afraid you can't let go? The Lord who made you wants to use you in ways you might never imagine. Ask Him to conquer the control freak in you. Today, practice turning something in your life over to God.

The point of conquering the control freak in us is

surrendering our hearts to God, and that might have to happen several times a day! Be alert to the surrendered heart in the verses below.

____

____

____

____

____

Meditate on These Verses:

> Proverbs 16:9, "In his heart a man plans his course, but the Lord determines his steps."
>
> Psalm 25:4 -5, "Show me your ways, O Lord, teach me your paths; guide me into your truth and teach me, for you are God my Savior, and my hope is in you all day long."

Challenge

We either love people, or we control them. There's little room for anything else. And it's far easier to control them than to love them. Start today to allow Jesus to be King in the areas of your struggle with control. What will you give back to God today?

____

____

____

____

____

____

Connect

Write back to God about your life, what you read, or a request on your heart.

____
____
____
____
____
____
____
____
____
____

Prayer

Father, teach me to follow and obey you. Your will is to restore things through your beloved Son, the King of Kings and Lord of Lords. Help us to break free from the enslavement of sin and be brought under your most gracious rule. Your ways are best. Amen.

Chapter 8: Glorified Dumpster Diver

"Then Mary took about a pint of pure nard, an expensive perfume; ***she poured it on Jesus' feet****..."* – John 12:3 (NIV)

I have been blessed to have many women in my life who believed in me. Whether I wanted it or not, I often found God placing women in my life for specific reasons and seasons. One such woman was Sue. She was an acquaintance at first through church who quickly became a mentor to me and a relationship I treasure. I can recall those first few invitations to her house for her weekly women's meetings. The hurt inside of me spoke volumes when I sharply lashed out at her, "Why would I do that? I don't even like women. They are mean and hurt each other. I am just fine the way I am." But "Coach," as I often referred to her, refused to give up on me. Using whatever tactics she could to entice me, she saw something in me that I didn't see in myself, and before long, her persistence worked.

At her house, I found a safe place of imperfect people with enormous hearts who welcomed and loved me. There I began to heal emotionally.

Sue was a garbage picker. OK, not really. She was really my mentor, but she claimed to be a glorified dumpster diver because of how she added women to her tribe.

Sue is an amazing woman, with a heart for God and a capacity to love the unlovable that warrants a tremendous platform. Her kindness and ability to deliver God's word are unmatched. But one thing that Coach always said about herself is that her calling, for that particular season of life, was as a glorified dumpster diver.

She clarified it by adding that she was someone who sought the discarded women of the world, the ones the church and society say don't measure up: the messed up, and spiritually disfigured, often at the hands of others. She found them and gently cleaned them up and helped to uncover the gifts of God inside them. She brought out the beautiful buried gems from under layers of shame and rejection.

Though Coach deserves a big stage, I believe she learned a secret that Mary of Bethany knew, as well. She allowed Jesus to lead her into unglamorous areas. She found that only when He leads do we find our true purpose. If we spend our lives chasing glitz, glamour and achievement that is not ours, we end up empty, alone and scorned.

Mary anointed Jesus feet. Again, we see a simple act with magnificent implications. Her deed, in essence, represented her desire for Jesus to lead her in her life on earth. Let God lead your life. Anoint His feet.

In doing this she signified that she would follow the feet that would be crucified for her. Jesus said, "Follow me," so she followed. Mary understood that the safest place was following Jesus closely. Wherever she saw His footsteps, she places her feet into His footprint. She was revealing, *"He is my leader. I get lost when I don't follow Jesus' footsteps."*

Once again, we see that Mary's actions were not random, but purposefully directed. In anointing Jesus' feet, she anointed Him as Lord of her life. The difference between Lord and King is that a Lord has a relationship with his servants. You honor your Lord and you allow them to guide you. A king is master over his subjects simply because of position. As King you honor and revere Him, as Lord you acknowledge His guidance in your relationship.

I learned this lesson's significance early on. As a young girl, I didn't get to see my grandfather often. He lived across the ocean and our times together were few and far between. But he was my hero. Grandpa was a great pioneer of the faith; I thought this was every girl's dream grandpa. On one of his evangelism trips to the United States, I got to spend some time with him on a farm while he ministered in the rural South.

During a rare afternoon off, Grandpa took this city girl through the woods and to the farm with a real cow, horse and pig. I was giddy and the excitement made time non-existent. When we approached the chickens, I felt that I could have lived in that coop. The farm animals were so cute; especially the chicks, and I thought how mean my parents were for never taking me to a place like this. Surely, they were holding out on me.

The darkness began to envelop us, slowly at first and without notice, then engulfing us. I can recall how complete the darkness was as we stepped out of the barn and yielded to the night's blackness. As our eyes adjusted, Grandpa reassured me and took out a small flashlight from his back pocket, as if he had known this might happen, and we began our trek back to the house through the bottomless, shadowy forest. I was so out of my element. I remember thinking that this was too scary a price to pay for a little time with some chickens, but I held back the tears so I wouldn't let Grandpa down. All I wanted was to be back home, safe and far away from all those strange sounds.

The thing I remember most about that journey through the dark forest was my grandfather's words to me. Step-by-step his words rang out rhythmically to me, "Just stay close behind me as I flash the light. Stay close. You won't be lost. Follow my feet. It's OK, I've got you. Stay close. I won't let you get hurt." No truer words had ever been spoken. The closer I followed behind, the safer I felt.

Jesus says the same words to us today. Whatever your darkness, whatever your scary situation, He whispers, "*Just stay close. It is going to be OK. Just stay close, I won't let you get hurt. Just stay close.*" The more we trust Jesus, and let Him lead us the safer we feel.

He longs to protect you, to lead you carefully in uncharted territories. He loves you so much and never wants to harm you. Let Him lead. He is the light. Follow Him close behind and you will stay secure. You don't have to see the whole plan, and you may not even understand why the portion of your life looks so dark. Stop focusing on your surroundings and just stay close. Anoint His feet and allow Him to lead.

Dig Deeper Devotion

Where can you follow Jesus more closely in your life? In what areas don't you let Jesus lead? How do you need to anoint His feet in your life?

Meditate on These Verses

> Psalm 25:4-5, *"Make me know Your ways, O LORD; Teach me Your paths. Lead me in Your truth and teach me, For You are the God of my salvation; For You I wait all the day."*
>
> Psalm 139:23-24, *"Search me, O God, and know my heart; Try me and know my anxious thoughts; And see if there be any hurtful way in me, And lead me in the everlasting way."*

Challenge

Where is God leading you? Where will you allow Him to lead you? Look for the "unglamorous" opportunities around you and follow closer in His footsteps for your purpose. Is the act of anointing His feet played out when we do what He is calling us to do in faith and boldness?

____

____

____

____

____

____

Connect

Write back to God about your life, what you read, or a request on your heart.

____
____
____
____
____
____

Prayer

Jesus, please help me to acknowledge you as my Lord. Help me to allow you to lead my life in areas where I am accustomed to leading myself. Guide my life. Amen.

Part Three

Gracious God – Changed Thinking

Chapter 9: Food Pantry Pride

"Then Mary took a pound of very costly oil of spikenard, anointed the feet of Jesus, ***and wiped His feet with her hair.*** *And the house was filled with the fragrance of the oil."* – John 12:3 (NKJV)

The reality of where I was standing was more than I thought I could handle. Waiting in a long line, tired, pregnant, and drained, the insult to my ego was harsh. I was heavily weighed down and not just because of my growing belly. I had come to the end of my resources and myself and had no choice but to get help.

With the rise and fall of the real estate roller coaster, that my husband and I happened to be riding in both directions, our outlook had now crashed. The ride was over when the roller coaster came to a screeching halt with what seemed like a sudden recession in 2007. All around our lives were remnants of what once was. Success, money, property, and prosperity had once been overflowing, but the rug had been pulled out from under us, and now our well of resources had run dry and my priorities quickly shifted to survival.

My family needed food, and we were also responsible for helping the congregants of our small church. School would be starting, and our kids had pretty slim pickings in their closet and pantry. So, I stood. Waited in line with others I had judged so quickly in the past. Now we were shoulder to shoulder with a similar goal: food and clothing.

Oh, how I'd taken for granted the "good" years; the overflow years, of the rise. Four years had passed as four days do, too busy to plan for tomorrow or what could happen. But growth often is accompanied with growing pains and that's where we were. Standing in line waiting for help, a real opposite of what we were used to, the helping others side of life.

I received two bags of groceries that day, some slightly expired, but all appreciated. And then the vouchers; they added insult to injury. We walked into a second hand store next to the food pantry and immediately were smacked with the smell of mustiness. And we were allowed to pick five items each of clothes or shoes. I wanted to leave that place so fast. What if any of my old clients saw me? What if the congregants that we always had a brave face for, saw me? If the earth had opened up in that second, I would have gladly jumped in.

But my children, the troopers they were, happily picked through the "new-to-them" racks as if searching for treasure. I was humiliated at first and then quickly humbled by the fact that I was no better than anyone else. We all go through seasons of drought in life. My pride took a severe blow that day as the realization kicked in that life changes quickly. I learned a valuable lesson that still resonates with me today. My pride belongs under my Master's feet. Just like Mary did.

The Bible teaches that a woman's hair is her glory (1 Corinthians 11:15). The visual message inherent in Mary's act of wiping Jesus' feet with her hair was one of humble service, submission, worship, and surrender.

Mary let down her hair and placed it under His feet, signifying that her glory was under His feet. How much pride do you take in your pride? Can you place it under His feet? I was ashamed to be standing in the food pantry lines, but necessity causes us to do unforeseen things.

Giving Up Self

Mary did something extremely scandalous, intimate and unthinkable. To unbind your hair and wipe someone's feet with it was not something respectful women did. Jewish women did not let down their hair in public. This is an expression of devotion that would have come across as improper. Mary was willing to do the work of a common slave for the Lord Jesus.

It appears that Mary was totally unselfconscious in her adoration and love of Jesus. She didn't care what others thought. Her primary focus was serving and honoring the Lord. She was not concerned with what anyone else thought. She had an undivided heart and a statement she needed to communicate to her master from the deepest part of her.

By doing what she did, Mary was demonstrating

that, *"If what's best for me conflicts with the glory of God, then I put it under Jesus feet."* This was one of the most powerful points she could make. His glory above my glory. Do we want our glory or God's glory?

Anointing the feet models service, discipleship, and love. In a culture in which a woman's touch was often forbidden, Mary dared to cradle the feet of Jesus in her hands and spread the oil across his ankles and toes with the ends of her hair.

Rather than measuring out a small amount of oil, Mary broke the jar and let it all pour out. She committed to be all-in, fully faithful, sparing no expense. This woman generously poured the oil she had reserved, without thought of the future.

A Public Display

Mary was not ashamed to make a spectacle of herself in showing her love for Jesus. Too often, we are afraid to show our love for Jesus in the workplace or the neighborhood for fear of being ridiculed for our faith.

We have all observed people in a public restaurant who wait until they think no one is looking and then quickly bow their heads for a few seconds to silently thank God for their food. Jesus warned, "For whoever is ashamed of Me and My words, of him the Son of Man will be ashamed when He comes in His own glory, and in His Father's, and of the holy angels" (Luke 9:26, NKJV).

When we come to sit at His feet, we will get to the place where we do not care what others may think of us. We will only have Him and His glory as the focus of our lives. He will fill our thoughts and our motives and we will lose sight of ourselves in the glorious light of His Person.

Mary showed by her example how to demonstrate a grateful heart for all that He has done for us, being totally uninhibited and unashamed in the expression of our love for Jesus. Therefore, we allow our pride to die and show a lost and dying world that we are not ashamed to worship, witness or work for the glory of Him who died to set us free. After all, our love for Him is in direct response to His love for us (1 John 4:19).

Falling Back at You

One more thing about Mary's experience; *the blessing came back on her own head.* When she broke the alabaster jar and anointed the feet of Jesus, she then wiped His feet with her hair.

We see in this act that the blessing and sweetness came back on her own head. In like manner when we pour out our prayers, love, and money to bless others, the blessing to a very great extent comes back into our own lives. This will continue to draw interest as long as we live here or hereafter.

The love that we pour out, comes back on our own heads. The tears you shed and the prayers you offer will come back to you. The life poured out will return like birds coming home to roost.

She wiped His feet with her hair; the *glory* of a woman. In total submission, Mary lay at His feet in willing worship. The odor of the spikenard filled the house. As she arose, the smell of the ointment was in her hair. Everywhere she went, it was a testimony that she had been with Jesus! *His glory* was all around her!

When Mary wiped Jesus' feet with her hair, she walked away smelling like Jesus did. **When we use what we have for Jesus, others can sense that we have been with Him.**

If your gift is mercy, you display the mercy that Jesus showed to us when He died in our place. If your gift is evangelism, then you display the love that Jesus has for sinners. The use of our spiritual gifts causes others to sense Jesus' presence in our lives.

I'm not going to suggest that there's a smell surrounding every person who is as close to the Lord as Mary was, but there is something – intangible possibly – something special about those who entertain Jesus in their hearts. And that something special spreads from them just like that sweet perfume that permeated that house.

Paul in his letter to the Philippians thanks them for their gifts to him and Timothy "...They are a **fragrant offering**, an acceptable sacrifice, pleasing to God" Philippians 4:18b, (NIV).

The offering of our lives to God, and through Him to others is just that – a fragrant offering, an acceptable sacrifice, pleasing to God. It's not about running around in circles trying to make sure our lives look busy and good. It's not about the value of the offering that we give. It's all about the attitude in which it is given, and the moment at which it is offered.

Compassionate Eyes

I believe when we struggle in an area of life, we respond one of two ways: fear or compassion. We either become so tight-fisted that we hoard our resources, love, and energy because of fear that one day we will lack again. Or we gain a change of perspective. We begin to see people not as they appear, but rather as they can be. We see others through eyes of compassion, relating to them because of our own experiences in food pantry lines.

I believe that is how Jesus saw people: through compassionate eyes of love, looking past the exterior, easy to judge, and into the hurt heart, the unspoken need crying out through desperate eyes. Standing in line for food taught me to see others differently. I remember seeing a homeless man soon after this experience. The corner was known for panhandlers, so I must have passed him a hundred times before, but this time I could not just look the other way.

My first thought this time was, *"How hard it must be for him, to hold up a sign and ask for help like this."* I went and bought him food and coffee with the change the kids and I could collect from the van and a few "emergency bucks" I had stashed and made a few U-turns to get back to him. I pulled over and left my girls glued to the windows as quietly observing participants. I walked across the road to the man and gave him the food and coffee. He thankfully grabbed the steaming cup and immediately began sipping what might as well have been liquid gold.

I remember the look of gratitude he exuded as he

told me how much he missed coffee. I managed only a few words, telling him that Jesus loves him, and he quickly replied that he was sure of that now, because Jesus had sent me to him. He answered questions that I had not asked out loud and began telling me his story. I left never looking at a needy person the same again. Aren't we all just a few turns of chance from his fate? If not "but by the grace of God".

Let us have a heart *that He may increase and I might decrease*. John 3:30 tells us, "He must become greater and greater, and I must become less and less" (NLT). Too many of us are OK with the part that he increases but not too many of us are OK with the part of us decreasing. We need to stop being a selfish generation. Stop blaming others for our own shortcomings and disappointments and realize that life does not revolve around us. We must put our glory under His feet.

The world defines success by what kind of car a person drives, what kind of clothes a woman wears, or what kind of house a family owns. With the Lord, it's not what kind of car a person drives; it's what kind of person drives the car. With God, the issue is what kind of woman wears the dress and what kind of family lives in the house. People look at the outward appearances, while God looks on the heart (1Samuel 16:7).

Mary's humility in anointing Jesus feet foreshadows the foot washing that is to come by Jesus for His disciples. As she has come to realize a bit more of the one who has been a friend to her and her siblings, her faith deepens and she recognizes her unworthiness. Her unpretentious act prepares us that Jesus will be all the more scandalized when He himself washes his disciples' feet and instructs them to do the same.

Mary's gesture was lavish, irrational, and apparently senseless. No wonder the disciples' reaction comes swiftly – what a waste! How much more practical it would have been to sell that expensive perfume – worth nearly a year's wages for a laborer – and to have used the money for something useful, like giving it to the poor! *Mary, what were you thinking?*

Maybe we can defend her, as Jesus did, by saying that her gesture made sense because she was in effect preparing his body for burial as some theologians suggest. But did Mary know what was to come? We will look at this in another chapter.

But I see more than that in this story. To me it is the very senselessness of this act of love that moves me most, for in a way every act of love is senseless. What is the point of love? What is the point of beauty? What is the point of existence itself? Mary's act of overflowing, extravagant love has no point in and of itself, just has love itself has no point in and of itself. And yet how beautiful it is, how necessary! It is an act that feeds the soul and an act by which we give ourselves to God.

When we begin to see how much Jesus suffered and paid for our sins, when we are genuinely converted from our selfish striving for recognition and grasping for earthly gain, then and *only then* will we be content to humbly serve and to give all to the One who gave all for us.

Dig Deeper Devotion

What are some areas of your life that you take great pride in (your kids, degree, house, etc.)? What would change in your perspective if your pride were suddenly broken? Let's recognize and voluntarily surrender our pride. Put our vanity under His feet and give that to Jesus. Ask Him to conquer the pride issues you struggle with in your life. Today, practice turning something in your life over to God. The point of conquering pride in our lives is surrendering our will to God's greater plan.

____
____
____
____
____
____
____
____
____
____
____
____
____

Meditate on These Verses

> John 3:30, "He must become greater and greater, and I must become less and less."

> Proverbs 29:23, "Pride ends in humiliation, while humility brings honor."

Challenge

Looking for our own glory sneaks into our lives. Starting today look for ways to humbly bring honor to God. Start with something small, such as ten minutes in prayer. Ask God to reveal areas of your life where you might need to surrender.

____

____

____

____

____

____

Connect

Write back to God about your life, what you read, or a request on your heart.

____

____

____

____

Prayer

Lord, help us to live unashamed. May our lives bring you glory and help us to put our pride daily under your feet. Amen.

Chapter 10: What's That Smell?

"Then Mary took a pound of very costly oil of spikenard, anointed the feet of Jesus, and wiped His feet with her hair. ***And the house was filled with the fragrance of the oil.****"* John 12:3 (NKJV)

I am so flawed. So far from perfect. I lose my temper too quickly (just ask my kids) I don't call my mom enough or ask about my mother-in-law's well-being as much as I should (ask either of them). I put my foot in my mouth all the time (ask my sisters). Just please don't ask my husband how "perfect" I am. After all, I have *some* dignity. A divide greater than the Grand Canyon are my flaws from God's standard. I don't always smell so good, but I endeavor to smell better day-by-day.

Onion Juice Hair is a Potent Reminder

I like to dabble. I also like Do-It-Yourself solutions and projects. So when I came across a remedy using something I already had in my home, to thicken my hair and get rid of stray grays, (not that I had any of those) I was more than intrigued. Why not? I really don't have much luck in the D-I-Y hair department, but this method looked easy enough. So I began.

The mixture called for chopping onion finely in a food processor and adding a bit of olive oil, and applying the concoction to my hair and letting it marinate twenty minutes. I could do this. So I did. Being the over-achiever, I am, I let the mixture sit for a few hours. The longer the better. No big deal. Only problem was that Pinterest doesn't mention that no matter how many times you shampoo the onion smell remains. For real!

I attempted four washes then five, and then I gave up, thinking I'd at least made a dent in the scent. Not so. My husband came up behind me and asked, "What's for dinner?" which quickly became the go-to jab he used for the next SIX weeks! Daily I received his comments of how delicious I smelled. I made him hungry. But I could not leave the house and be in close quarters with anyone without hearing, "What's that smell?"

Onion odor followed me like a lonely puppy only I could not shake it. And Heaven help us if it was hot. Sweat exacerbated the stench. And I could not hide. I look back now and laugh, but truthfully the scent was overpowering.

Overwhelming Scent

Have you ever experienced a fragrance overwhelming you? Where a door has been opened, a meal has been put before you, or a breeze has come from an unexpected direction, and you are flooded by memory?

Smell is so entwined with remembrance. It is one of the primary triggers for memory. For centuries we have known that odors have a significant impact on how we feel. Humans have the capability to distinguish about 10,000 different smells. Smell is the most powerful sense for bringing back memories because the olfactory bulb in the brain's limbic system which is the part of the brain that controls our moods, emotions, memory and learning. And how the brain forever links the scent of freshly-cut roses to the security of your grandmother's guest room. Lavender reduces stress. Jasmine relaxes. Lemon stimulates. Odors do make a difference.

Scent, unlike anything else, invokes memories. Aroma unites the senses of taste, touch, sight, and sound to place us, at least for a moment, in a time past.

In contrast to the great importance placed on all other senses, smell is the most evocative of all our senses, reaching the deepest parts of ourselves, bypassing our rational understanding and going straight to the most elemental, instinctive part of ourselves, awakening deep memories or opening up new realms in our imaginations.

I have always been captivated by fragrance. Ordering essential oils is not an uncommon practice in my world. I became a quick student of aromatherapy, which means "treatment using scents". It is a way of caring for the body with pleasant smelling oils. The essential oils are added to a bath or massaged into the skin, inhaled directly or diffused to scent an entire room. Aromatherapy is used to relieve pain, care for the skin, alleviate tension and fatigue and invigorate the entire body.

Smells can fill a space, in pleasant and unpleasant ways, much like light and sound, transmitting barely-visible particles from their origin to deep into our bodies. Smell transcends time and space with an immediacy that no other sense can match.

Of all the senses, smell could be the one we are least likely to engage when we read, least of all the Bible. But imagine the many smells evoked throughout the Old and New Testaments. The smell of fine poured wine. The odor of a pallet of a man who has been lying paralyzed for nearly forty years. The fragrance of bread just pulled from the oven. The odor of mud, just created from dirt and spit, rubbed on a blind man's eyes. The waft of a body four days dead. Smells can gratify *and* repulse, delight and distance, anticipate and repel. Yet smell is a very human part of life especially for women, who are more sensitive to it.

Connecting to Jesus' Scent

I got excited thinking about making that deepest of sense connections with the place where Jesus was that night. Because, even though the house itself can no longer be seen, the voices of Jesus and his friends cannot be heard today, the dinner can never be eaten again, and the feeling of Mary's hair wiping in the spikenard can never be felt exactly in the same way, the two things that still exist about that night, besides the eternal living Christ, are what was written about it and this particular scent.

When we smell spikenard's earthy tone, we smell the same scent that Jesus smelled that night, a smell that no doubt stayed with him through that last, memorable week of His life on earth. Through this scent, we enter into the mind of Christ in a way no other experience can.

Take a moment just to be with Jesus in this time and place. Imagine experiencing Him. See the light, flickering low that evening, lighting less of the house than the smell would reach. Envision those surprised guests who thought they saw something wasteful, when actually they saw Jesus being prepared for death while living.

The obvious smell of the "costly perfume made of pure spikenard," that Mary anoints Jesus' feet with make Judas irate. This anointing is important. Anointing had one of two connotations. It was either typically associated with kingship and the head was anointed, or it was applied to a body after death. So Mary's anointing of Jesus' feet carries an additional clue as to how Mary perceived her Lord. At the same time, feet in the ancient world were always quite dirty as the main shoes were sandals, and the streets were quite dusty. Mary's attention for Jesus' feet was a deeply loving act of care and devotion. Let the senses of this scene come alive to you as we read this passage from John 12: 1-8.

"Six days before the Passover celebration began,
Jesus arrived in Bethany, the home of Lazarus—the
man he had raised from the dead. [2]A dinner was
prepared in Jesus' honor. Martha served, and Lazarus
was among those who ate with him. [3]Then Mary took a
twelve-ounce jar of expensive perfume made from
essence of nard, and she anointed Jesus' feet with it,
wiping his feet with her hair. The house was filled with
the fragrance."[4]But Judas Iscariot, the disciple who
would soon betray him, said, [5]"That perfume was worth
a year's wages. It should have been sold and the money
given to the poor." [6]Not that he cared for the poor—he
was a thief, and since he was in charge of the disciples'
money, he often stole some for himself. [7]Jesus replied,
"Leave her alone. She did this in preparation for my
burial. [8]You will always have the poor among you, but
you will not always have me."

In the upside-down Kingdom of Jesus, this story makes perfect sense.

What's That Smell

"The house was filled with the fragrance of the perfume," John tells us. This got me wondering, – "What is spikenard? And what does nard smell like?" What did it smell like in Lazarus' house that night after dinner, as Mary anointed Jesus' feet? Perhaps the smell of grilled lamb still hanging in the air, mixed with that spikenard perfume? A quick search tells me that nard, the full name being "spikenard," is an amber-colored essential oil derived from a flowering plant of the Valerian family that grows in the Himalayas of Nepal, China, and India. Nard is thick in consistency and comes in many different varieties, some of which smell slightly like lavender. I imagine there were good smells in Lazarus' house that night – perhaps of freshly baked bread, the smoke of a wood fire after dinner, mixed in with the fragrance of earthy, musky, lavender.

John paints an intimate picture for us of Jesus and his disciples gathered together to share a meal and fellowship with one another along with Lazarus, Mary, and Martha. We get an image of comfort, warmth, and love. We almost feel like we are there. How awesome it would've been to be there with Jesus and to enjoy all of those good smells!

But then Judas interrupts this heartfelt, intimate scene with an unsettling question. *"Why was this perfume not sold for three hundred denarii and the money given to the poor?"* Judas stinks. Not literally, necessarily, but something about Judas doesn't smell quite right, if you will. He's a thief – he doesn't really care about the poor, and as the group's treasurer he steals from their collected offerings instead of giving them to the poor. We know just a few days later he'll betray Jesus and hand Him over to be put to death by the Roman authorities for thirty pieces of silver. In contrast to the fragrance of Mary's loving devotion and anointing of Jesus, Judas stinks of greed and betrayal, self-interest instead of self-sacrifice for the sake of Jesus and His mission.

So, what do *we* smell like? This isn't a question to make us feel self-conscious. What I mean is, in the way we live our daily lives, in the way we welcome and offer hospitality, can people "smell" the fragrance of Christ, or do we come across as disingenuous, insincere, or even self-serving, like Judas?

The apostle Paul in 2 Corinthians 2:15-16 wrote, "For we are the aroma of Christ to God among those who are being saved and among those who are perishing; to the one a fragrance from death to death, to the other a fragrance from life to life." I have always liked this idea that as Christians the fragrance of Christ rubs off of Him and onto us as we grow deeper in relationship with Him. The fragrance of death, the smell of Judas's inauthentic and self-serving faith stank more like a pile of garbage, as one of Jesus' closest disciples delivered Him over to the soldiers for thirty pieces of silver. Mary anointed Jesus for his burial, so that the smell of death, the smell of Judas' betrayal, would be overpowered by the extravagant fragrance of spikenard.

The House was Filled with the Fragrance

Several immediate results from Mary's worship were apparent. The fragrance of her offering filled the room. There was a change in the atmosphere! In the same way, when we pour out all in worship to Jesus the beauty of that offering can be sensed by those around us.

It is an Alluring Fragrance that Lingers

Acts 4:13 says, "The members of the council were amazed when they saw the boldness of Peter and John, for they could see that they were ordinary men with no special training in the Scriptures. They also recognized them as men who had been with Jesus." (NLT) Peter and John amazed the Pharisees with their courage because they spoke with power, and the Pharisees noted that these men had been with Jesus. Do we leave such an impression on others?

Mary and the disciples, in spending time with Jesus, in listening and following His teachings, were with Jesus so often and so closely that the fragrance of Christ permeated through every pore so pungently. Even after Jesus' death, resurrection and ascension, Christ's aroma continued to be with them as they formed the early church and started to bring the good news of Christ to other communities around the world. When they encountered others, even though Jesus was not physically present, unbelievers could "smell" who Christ was. Our Messiah's fragrance was powerful enough for the aroma of Christ to draw others, so that the church grew.

It's interesting, isn't it, how powerful the sense of smell can be? One whiff of a certain perfume might remind us of an aunt, our moms, or a strict teacher. Mary's anointing of Jesus caused the room to be filled with a fragrance of Christ that ALL present would remember. They would smell spikenard as Jesus entered Jerusalem. They would smell it as he prayed with them in the Garden of Gethsemane and again as He carried his cross to Golgotha. Perhaps even before they saw the stone rolled away and found the empty tomb, would they smell Christ's presence again that resurrection morning? They smelled and remembered his teachings, recalled how he healed those who were sick and how

He loved them.

When people come into contact with us, do they smell the aroma of Christ? Do they leave with the scent of welcome, of genuine hospitality, with memories of prayers of joy and worries shared? Do they have a sense of security, that with us it's OK to both laugh and cry, to wrestle with the questions of belief, and to be inspired by powerful faith stories? It should smell like Jesus when people interact with us. It should smell like the aroma of Christ. And I hope that when we all go about our daily lives, that same fragrance of Christ goes with us and lingers when we leave a room. May the aroma of Christ that we see and experience in these pages sink deep into our pores, so that people can't help but notice that we smell like Christians.

Worship Jesus. When we are with Him, the fragrance of his love fills our hearts and spills over. The atmosphere changes within us and around us. Just as the Pharisees did, people today can tell when we have been around Jesus.

Mary's Love Offering Lingered

What does Jesus want of us more than anything? He doesn't need our money and doesn't want our things. Jesus desires our love. Jesus wants our hearts. We give our complete focus, our resources, our hearts, and our unconditional surrender when we truly fall in love with Jesus.

Our adoration is the one thing He can't claim without our offering it to Him. Jesus longs for us to come close to Him. He wants us to worship through our struggle.

Our response to being loved, chosen, and known is worship. How does our worship smell?

Worshiping with the right attitude in our hearts changes things. Worship changes the atmosphere; it changes our hearts; it changes our lives. And people will know we have been with Jesus in worship. Worship is like pouring all we are on Him like oil in an uneven divine exchange. Adore him. Let His scent linger on you.

Notice the Fragrance

When Mary broke the alabaster jar and poured it on Jesus, the house, we are told, was filled with the sweet odor. When Jesus poured out His life on Calvary, earth and Heaven were filled with the fragrance of His life. The fragrant oil that Mary poured out is a metaphor for the Holy Spirit. The Holy Spirit brings to us the very fragrance and sweetness of Heaven.

There is something about the sanctified, Spirit-filled life, which cannot be captured in words. It is the breath of Jesus in the heart, the vapor from the river of life. The fragrance of such a life soon permeates the home, motivates the church, distributes itself through the community, and even goes around the world.

Many never experience the fullness of God's peace and power because they surrender only partially to Him. The Lord can fill our vessels only to the extent that we empty them.

Is the Lord asking all of us to liquidate 100 percent of our assets and give them as an offering? Not necessarily, but He is asking us to put everything on the altar and then be willing to do whatever He directs. He is asking for a no-strings-attached commitment.

Without Christ, our lives carry the stench of death. We cannot come into our Heavenly Father's presence because of that putrid smell clinging to us. But when God forgives us of our sins and we place our faith in Jesus, we are wrapped in the robes of Christ: ***we smell like Him and are welcomed into the Father's presence.***

The Gift of Smell Lingers

"The house was filled with the fragrance...," says the gospel.

What does it smell like? What would Mary smell? Not necessarily what you might expect a perfume to smell like, if your expectations are of a floral garden. Spikenard has a profound and complex aroma, a combination of sweet, spicy, and musky. Nard has an organic earthy scent. It is a smell bursting with life and promise.

Mary did not count the cost; she never seemed to care about the cost. She was totally oblivious to what others were thinking when she was with Jesus. As far as Mary was concerned no one else was there, no one else mattered but her Lord.

Mary showed absolute adoration, beyond ritual, beyond liturgy, beyond all practicality. This is the way to come to Jesus. And Jesus tells us this is the way He wants us to come to the poor, to love the unlovable and to love each other – extravagantly and beyond all practicality.

At this last oasis on His journey to the cross, Jesus is

loved, truly loved, in the manner He deserves. He was loved while He was with Mary, and He would soon be gone.

What does God Smell Like?

As I mentioned earlier, I appreciate essential oils, so much that I often carry small vials of select oils in my purse. Recently I didn't close the peppermint oil well, and a few drops leaked out into my purse. Wipe as I may, the smell of those few drops lasted and lasted. Weeks later, I still am welcomed with the aroma of peppermint when I scrounge through my purse. I am fascinated by how long certain smells can linger. And I am reminded of generous Mary and her pouring the oil to anoint Jesus.

Spikenard is described as "intensely aromatic." So, we're talking about a pungent ointment to begin with, but notice the verse says she used an entire pound of it. I have learned that a little goes a long way with essential oils. I cannot imagine using a pound of any of these oils. I typically use a few drops. But a pound? We know it was fragrant because the verse goes on to say the entire house was filled with the odor, and it probably remained that way for some time.

Another thing I've learned about essential oils is that their fragrance remains even after washing. It's difficult to eliminate the smell. With that thought in mind, isn't it possible that Jesus had the odor of spikenard clinging to Him as He walked up the long road to Calvary? As He hung on that old rugged cross, could He still smell the fragrance on His skin? And when the Father turned away from His own Son, did the smell of spikenard remind Christ that He was loved? Someone loved Him enough to anoint Him with oil. Did the scent bring Him a sense of peace during a time of such agony? He thought it was a beautiful thing.

Not only that, but Mary bore the fragrance as well. I imagine the smell lingered with her for several days. But I don't think Mary minded. After all, she smelled like Jesus. The aroma reminded her of her Lord and Savior. The fragrance brought with it the bittersweet thoughts of His sacrifice on the cross and His conquering of the grave.

The Enduring Fragrance of a Poured-Out Life

The lingering effect of her poured out life causes me to hunger for the same sacrificial kind of worship. I can smell the fragrance of worship. I draw in the scent of sacrifice. I breathe the bouquet of brokenness. I waft the perfume of a life that was poured out. I can inhale the pleasing aroma of the posture of her heart that says no cost is too great if it's for the Lord Jesus Christ.

May we each live lives that are broken and spilled out and may each of our homes be filled with the perfume of the King. He is worthy to be worshiped. He is worthy to be exalted. He is worthy of all glory and honor.

Dig Deeper Devotion

Mary had spent enough time with Jesus and drawn so close to Him in her worship that she literally smelled like Him. What about us? Do we carry with us the fragrance of love, goodness and mercy? Or do we reek from the stench of hatefulness, bitterness and pride? When we walk past others, can they tell that we've been with Jesus? Do they see His light in our eyes? Do they hear His words on our lips? Do they feel His love in our actions? Do we smell like Jesus today? Are others attracted to the aroma of Christ because of what they smell in us? Smelling good honors the work Jesus did on the Cross.

____

____

____

____

____

____

____

____

Meditate on These Verses

> Ephesians 5:2, "Live a life filled with love, following the example of Christ. He loved us and offered Himself as a sacrifice for us, a pleasing aroma to God."

> 2 Corinthians 2:14-15, "Now [God] uses us to spread the knowledge of Christ everywhere,

like a sweet perfume. Our lives are a Christ-like fragrance rising up to God…"

Challenge

How does your sense of smell, or your other senses, help you on your journey of faith? What scents particularly make you come alive, or link you to other times and places?

____
____
____
____
____

Connect

Write back to God about your life, what you read, or a request on your heart.

____
____
____
____
____

Prayer

Lord, help us to pour out our lives before you. May we draw others into your knowledge because they are attracted to the scent of Jesus on and in us. Amen.

Chapter 11: Necessary Forced Perspective Change

"Leave her alone, why are you bothering her? ***She has done a beautiful thing to me.****"* - Mark 14:6 NLT

Dog shaming cracks me up. I know I shouldn't find it as funny as I do, but seeing those innocent puppy eyes behind a sign that tells of their misdeeds is absolutely hysterical to me. You have probably seen them on social media and LOLed, too. Some of my favorites include, "I only chew up the left shoes", and "I eat crayons and poop rainbows," and great big puppy dog eyes with a sign around his neck reading, "I break into the pantry and hide potatoes all around the house."

What if we unknowingly place signs on others to shame them? What labels have I put on that athletic, put-together woman strutting her way down the street? What sign have I placed around her neck based on my own perception and nothing that has to do with her? What about the sign I have placed on the woman who just served me from behind a counter? Her disheveled and worn appearance allows me to quickly label her, freeing me to move on without consideration for the human behind the uniform.

Jesus looked at the heart and motivation of an individual, not at the outward appearance. When we begin to look at people with eyes of kindness, we start to see them differently. Everyone you meet is battling something you know nothing about.

What if I began to see people with Jesus's eyes? My rebellious teenager with the smart mouth and sharp tongue would look a lot like a hurt, scared little girl trying to find her identity. My neighbor with the immaculate house and lawn would look like a struggling woman tired of the competition. The woman at the check-out line ahead of us who just yelled at her kids wouldn't look as much an unfit mother, but a lot like you and me.

Jesus's eyes saw Mary of Bethany differently. While others quickly judged her worship, Jesus commended her extravagance and said she knew something others didn't.

Hiding Behind a Smile

My parents did the best they knew in raising us. I was

their first experience with children, and in a foreign country, they simply winged it many times. Hence my kindergarten pictures. They assumed it was a way bigger deal than it was, and I showed up in an elaborate white dress complete with netting underneath to puff it up. The beautifully stitched butterfly on the bright red chest piece competed for attention with my face, which was pretty dolled up. My mom thought it would be a good idea to put a full face of makeup on her six-year-old. So my bright red lipstick, rosy cheeks, and blue eye shadow completed the look with my teased hair. It was a sight for certain. Not knowing any different, I enjoyed getting dolled up and marched myself to school only to find that nobody was that dressed up but me. My pictures show a chubby doll faced mini-adult who was hiding deep secrets and hurts under her practiced smile. I had invisible signs I was holding up too. “Responsible,” “Mature,” “Obedient,” but inside I cried out for love, safety and understanding.

We label and are labeled. Jesus has come to see past all labels. Just as He saw past the labels others applied to Mary of Bethany, He understood her pure intentions; He wants to do the same for us as well.

Mary was the listener, the emotional one, the sensitive soul. Mary took a jar of expensive perfume and fell at Jesus’ feet as if she knew something that other people didn’t fully realize. Mary sensed in that moment, she wanted to do something special for Jesus. She was doing the right thing toward Jesus at the right time. Some people have that gift: the gift of doing the right thing for someone at the right moment. Some of you have that gift, the ability to recognize the sacredness of a moment and to do the right thing. Mary did.

Good Gifts

You see, a really good gift will say more about the recipient receiving it than it does about the giver. The gift itself speaks to who the person is. Some of you are really good at giving this kind of gift. You pay attention to what your friend likes and you find just the thing that they would appreciate. The gift shows that you have seen them, that you know them, that you honor them. Mary of Bethany was seeing something of Jesus and honoring Him through her gift in a way that others around her were not. Mary did the sensitive thing at the right moment, sharing her love and thanksgiving for Jesus, even though she would be condemned for it.

What was Mary's motivation to do this sacred undertaking? Maybe her deep love and affection for Jesus grew from their relationship wherein Jesus had taught her so much about God and agape, undeserved love. Maybe her deep affection was because Jesus had given her brother Lazarus back to her. Maybe her deep affection is that she loved Jesus and knew He was going to die very soon, and she wanted to make a last loving gesture to Him. We don't know what her motives were.

Perhaps her deep affection for Jesus was grounded in all of these things. What we do know is that Mary made a gift of herself, an extravagant gift of love for Jesus that we are all called to emulate. Although others judged her, she didn't shrink back from her devotion.

What kind of devotion, what kind of love, causes

someone to do something like that – to first of all enter a place where she is most likely not welcome, to pour out the equivalent of a year's wages, to endure the rebuke of those who would not understand, and the indignation of those who would think she had totally missed the point of Jesus's ministry.

Extravagant Exchange

Well, Jesus had raised her brother from the dead. What kind of gift do you give to someone who has not just saved your beloved brother's life but actually brought him back to life after death? In that context, $40,000 is nothing. Those of us who have lost a loved one understand. I would certainly give $40,000 to bring my dad or niece back. If you've ever received an undeserved or lavish gift, as a pure gift, you know the desire that rises up in you to give something in return out of gratitude. You know you could never repay the gift but you want your thank you to be really fitting for the gift you received. If we think of it in that way, maybe her extravagant gift doesn't seem so crazy after all.

But still, even if we understand her motives and can identify with her desire to show her gratitude and devotion, it still seems like a waste, does it not? Jesus knew He was approaching death, couldn't He at least have done like many people now do at funerals, "In lieu of flowers – or extravagant perfume as this case may be – the family would like to suggest you make a donation to his favorite charity."

Couldn't Jesus have stopped her *before* she

broke the jar, told her how much he appreciated the gesture, reminded her that whatever she did for the least she did for Him and asked her to go sell the perfume and go give it to the poor in His name?

Yet, Jesus doesn't seem to blink an eye when she breaks the jar. He doesn't stop her or patronize, as if to pat her on the head and say, "That's a sweet gesture, my friend, but what I really want is...." No, there must be some reason that He let her continue. Maybe He knew this scent would be a light that would carry Him through the dark days ahead. Or, maybe being anointed confirmed in Him His calling to be obedient, even to the point of death.

How appropriate to anoint Jesus as He faced this call to bring healing to the world through death. He had been hinting at this for days already with His disciples but none of them seemed to get it. Finally, here was someone who seemed to understand that he was facing death, someone who not only understood but actually anointed Him for it, blessing Him in it. Mary was giving Him not only a gift of gratitude, but also a gift of understanding, a gift of honoring His call, a gift to strengthen, a gift to bless, a gift of devotion and love as He prepared to face His betrayers, angry mobs and power-hungry officials. "She has done a beautiful thing to me."

Change your Perspective

While scrolling through social media, I stumbled on some neat forced perspective pictures. These photos show a person holding the moon in his hand or crushing the Eiffel Tower between her thumb and forefinger. I wondered if sometimes I need to force my perspective to change as well. Those times when I'm feeling down or blue. Those times when I'm feeling less than others. Do I need to force my perspective to change? Those times, so frequently, when I am quick to defend my actions, yet I am called to be quiet instead. Sometimes we need to look at things differently in order to have a different outcome in life. We need to force our perspective to change from the defender to the defendant.

Turn your Pain into Purpose

Periods of our lives that cause us great pain and make easy targets for the judgment of others, can either make us bitter or better. That deep sorrow you are dealing with, that addiction you are overcoming, the debt that hasn't choked you yet, the disease you battle with daily, for example, can either make you bitter, as the enemy wants, or it can become your entry point to the ministry you are called for. If you allow it.

Your pain becomes your podium, your place, from experience, to speak hope and encouragement to someone in the thick of despair. Often people will not allow access into certain painful parts of life, because of fear: fear of judgment, misunderstanding or not being related to.

But when you can show them that you have been there, or are currently there, all of a sudden you are granted access to that area. Your pain becomes the passport, gaining access to uncharted territories of another's agony. Your suffering becomes your stage on which you have the credibility to speak reassurance and courage to another.

Your passport into people's paths is your pain. "Do I have your permission to cross your border? No? Well, let me show you my passport."

I recall a story someone told me of a stubborn old donkey. That animal had seen better days, and its health and usefulness seemed long past. Its owner had grown fond of the donkey's persistent attitude and could not bring himself to shoot it so he decided he would just have the poor thing thrown down an abandoned well shaft that they threw trash into. Troubled, and true to the donkey's persevering nature, it daily waited for the trash to be thrown in and the donkey tenaciously sifted through what it could eat for nourishment and simply stomped on the rest. Day after day this continued until one day, months later, that stubborn donkey unassumingly climbed his way out of the pit and walked back to its owner, as if to say, *"All that trash you threw at me helped me get out of my pit!"*

What a lesson we can learn from that donkey. Will we allow the trash that the world throws at us to bury us or will we allow it to become the thing that gets us out of the pit we are in? Stomp, sweet sister. Don't lie down and die! Don't be defined by your circumstances. Allow your source of pain to become your platform and start speaking life to others.

Mary Didn't Fight for Her Rights

We can choose to defend ourselves in life, or we can let Jesus defend us. When Martha reprimanded Mary in front of others and demanded that Jesus order her to help, did Mary have the right to speak back? (Luke 10:38-42) I believe she did have that right. But she didn't speak up. Mary's focus was undivided. She wasn't lazy; she was captivated. She was doing the one thing required: loving Jesus. It takes more strength not to talk. When she was quiet… Jesus answered! Mary's defense was greater when Jesus spoke for her. Like a good defense attorney speaks with authority on behalf of the accused, so Jesus defends us if we choose to let Him. Mary didn't fight for her rights. She let Jesus defend her!

Make A Statement

What impresses us about the record of Mary anointing Jesus is the absence of any conversation. Mary said nothing! While the others sat at the table, Mary was at her accustomed place at the feet of Jesus. In Martha's house, Mary listened, and was silent; at her brother's grave she wept. In the house of Simon, she worshiped and was quiet. In fact, the only time Mary said anything at all was when she repeated the complaint of Martha in Luke 11:32. Silent love can be a mighty force. The greatest work in the world is not always accomplished by the best speakers.

Mary was so absorbed in the joy of serving Jesus that she was oblivious to the stunned reactions of the guests seated around the table. After she broke open the alabaster flask, the room quickly filled with the profusion of a costly, exotic essence. The conversation in the room probably quieted to a tense murmur. Mary surely felt the piercing stares of all present.

Mary's genuine sacrifice and service was a stinging rebuke to the selfishness of Judas in John 12:3-6. Immediately after his pious statement of concern for the poor, Judas went out and agreed to betray the Savior for the price of a slave. Judas, pretending to be indignant, protested under his breath – just loud enough for those seated nearby to hear. "*What a tragic waste of resources!*" he exclaimed. "*Why, this oil could have been sold for more than three hundred denari.*" Then, as an afterthought to cloak his own greedy plans, Judas added: "*Of course, the proceeds could have been donated to the poor!*"

Judas seems to have his own notion of who Jesus should be. Rather than truly looking and seeking to understand Jesus, he decided he could not offer Jesus his devotion and went right out after this event to betray Him. Judas selfish heart had felt keenly rebuked by Mary's liberal generosity.

Often those who look down their noses at "sinners" are, like Judas, doing this as a diversionary tactic to distract from their own sins. The most critical and judgmental people in the church are usually the ones who are struggling the most with hidden guilt.

Jesus Defends the Worshiper

Because Mary was not afraid to openly demonstrate her

loyalty and submission to Jesus, the Lord, was likewise willing to defend her in front of others. Jesus heard His faithful disciples echo Judas's murmurings. With sad compassion, He said to them: *"Why do you trouble the woman? For she has done a good work for Me. For you have the poor with you always, but Me, you do not have always. For in pouring this fragrant oil on My body, she did it for My burial."*

Of course, we need to care for the poor. After all, Jesus himself came to embrace the lost and lonely and marginalized, and to set the captive free. In Matthew's gospel, Jesus even tells us that he so identifies with the poor, that when we feed and clothe the poor, we feed and clothe Jesus Himself. (Matthew 25:31-45)

Yet in this story, Jesus lifts up another truth. There comes a time when we must set aside being efficient, useful, and sensible. Mary's story reminds us that every genuine act of love, however muddled – every gesture of kindness, however incoherent – every act of creativity, however wild and extravagant it might be – can be our offering to God, our way of giving thanks and sharing in God's love.

The clear statement of Jesus's approval must have brought great joy to Mary's heart. Knowing that the Lord was pleased with her was all she ever wanted. Jesus was protective of Mary because He understood her heart. Throughout Scripture, women characters are often symbolic of the church, and flawed and defective though she might appear, Jesus is grieved and angered by those who stand by and accuse the bride of Christ, like Judas did.

When Jesus defended Mary, he wasn't placating

her. He wasn't saying, "Be nice to her. She has good intentions and that's what matters." This is not an individualistic story about tolerance like we hear today, like, "Let's just let everyone do their own thing. It's the intention that counts."

We know this because Jesus does not always respond in this way. To the rich young ruler, Jesus said, "Go sell your possessions," which would have included any expensive perfume he would have, and give it to the poor. To Peter, who in his own act of devotion told Jesus he would not let Him suffer and die, Jesus' gave a firm response: "Get behind me Satan". Peter wanted Jesus to do something Jesus was not called to; Peter's was an act of misplaced devotion.

Mary, on the other hand, recognizes and accepted Jesus's calling and recognized who He was. Her act of devotion shed light on that. Mary truly exalted Him, not her own agenda, not her own desired view of Jesus, but for who Jesus really was: a king, but the unheard-of type of king that would allow Himself to be anointed by a woman. Who would dismantle oppressive power structures such as patriarchy rather than upholding them. An honored prophet who deserved lavish gifts, but one who would sit in solidarity with the outcasts such as lepers and women. A priest, but One who offered his very own life to be poured out in sacrifice.

Mary's gift itself was a symbol that pointed to the gift that Jesus would offer the world. Jesus was a lavish gift of pure spikenard about to be broken open and poured out, filling not just one room but the whole world with the sweet scent of his offering. The world would never smell the same again. In response to this gift from Jesus, we, too, are invited to offer our lives as a lavish gift, to be poured out in devotion to God so that our world may also be filled with the fragrance of Christ.

"Leave her alone, why are you bothering her? She has done a beautiful thing to me... But you will not always have me. She did what she could... Wherever the gospel is preached..." Mark 14:6–9 (NLT).

Jesus defended Mary's reckless worship. He understood the depths of her love. "She did a beautiful thing to me." Jesus did not utter such words of praise about anyone else in Scripture. She spent all her love on Him.

Maybe your motives have been misunderstood. Maybe you've been criticized for your worship, your ministry, or what you believe. We are hurt by others and we hurt others. We can talk about it and complain, or Jesus can resolve it for us. The choice is ours. What did Mary do? She let Jesus defend her! Jesus always defends a worshiper. May we learn that we need not shield ourselves. Let the Master defender defend us.

Dig Deeper Devotion

Is there a gift you can give Jesus that speaks of Him, that honors who He is regardless of what others say about you? What kind of gift would speak of your devotion to the One who journeyed toward death on our behalf? What kind of lavish gifts could we offer those who struggle around us, and through them offer to Jesus, that honors them in their journey? Is it something practical? Is it the gift of presence? Is it to anoint their heads with an abundance of prayer? Is it to offer them the gift of support?

____

____

____

____

____

____

____

Meditate on These Verses

> Exodus 14:14, "The Lord will fight for you, and you shall hold your peace."

> Psalm 43:1, "Declare me innocent, O God! Defend me against these ungodly people. Rescue me from these unjust liars."

Challenge

Have you been forced to carry a sign around your neck that proclaims something to the world other than what's in your heart? Ask Jesus to reveal to your heart how He sees you.

____

____

____

____

Connect

Write back to God about your life, what you read, or a request on your heart.

____

____

____

____

Prayer

Jesus, I ask for the gift to sit, like Mary at your feet, to be reminded of all of the ways that you have given me new life, the ways that you have shown me your love. What gift of devotion can I offer you that would bring you honor, that would speak to who you are, that would be a beautiful thing to you? Show me how to glorify You regardless of what others may think. Amen.

Chapter 12: Death is a Tool

"Then said Jesus, Let her alone: ***against the day of my burying*** *hath she kept this."* - John 12: 7 KJV

Naming Grace

By the amount of activity in my belly, I was certain that my second child would be a boy. This baby didn't stop kicking and punching, which brought extra pregnancy exhaustion. Each ultrasound brought more uncertainty. This child didn't stop long enough for them to determine the gender. That was until the final ultrasound before my delivery was to take place. I had requested this appointment because I wanted a natural birth after an extremely hard C-section delivery with my first child. So the ultrasound was scheduled to see how big the baby was and possibly see the gender this time.

I knew something wasn't quite right when the technician started to pause and hmm a lot. I asked what was wrong. She didn't answer and said she'd be right back. What seemed like eons passed before the doctor hurried back into the room and began ultrasounding my belly herself. She quickly explained how this baby was certainly a girl and she had a large tumor in one of her ovaries. I still remember the heaviness that seemed to compress my chest as I struggled to catch my breath. They would need to do an emergency C-section and she would have to have surgery a few days after birth. My husband supported me as I walked out of the room, reeling from the revelation, inconsolable, my head swimming with what-if scenarios.

My big fat Egyptian family and I arrived bright and early the next morning for the surgery, and my support team of twenty remained anxiously in the waiting room. When they delivered the baby, once again I knew something wasn't quite right. Instead of bringing her to me to bond with and take pictures, they quickly thrust her up and showed me her bluish hued form in a flash, saying, "Here she is" and scurried with her over where I could barely see the hustle around her. I remember repeating to my husband over and over, "Why isn't she crying? I can't hear her. What's wrong?! Go see!" The doctors stabilized me, and my husband went with the baby. I drifted in and out of consciousness for some time. When I awoke, all I could utter was, "Where is she?" I wanted to see my baby. They sent for my husband and he explained that when this baby was born, the umbilical cord was wrapped so tightly around her neck that she was not breathing. The doctors had to intubate her and put our baby on a breathing machine, but she was a fighter. The doctor also told me that had I tried to deliver her naturally, she would not have survived. Funny how God works sometimes.

Nurses wheeled my bed into a room that had another woman and her baby in it. I sobbed, longing to hold my own bundle of joy. I was not allowed to move, still numb from surgery, so I could not see my baby until the next day when I could manage to get up from the massive surgery. I was in despair. Raging hormones mixed with confusion. I had to face the barrage of well-meaning visitors. My father was my strength that day, limiting visitors and shooing everyone out of the room when he could tell I couldn't take it. I remember him sitting at the foot of the bed and asking me what we were going to name this spunky one. I told him I had no girl names, as I was convinced we were having a boy. Dad simply nodded, and asked in his thick Middle-Eastern accent, "What about Grace? This baby is going to be God's grace expressed for our family." All of a sudden there were no other options.

Baby Grace pulled out the intubation tube that evening and began miraculously breathing on her own. She amazed the Neonatal Intensive Care Unit nurses and our family, and she still does. She graced her way through surgery at seven days old, and I scarcely left her side at that NICU. Leaving her there felt like my heart was being ripped out daily. So it became a second home until she was released. She continued to represent God's favor at every milestone. The doctors had said they would have to remove her ovary. Instead, they were able to save it, and she is a healthy young lady today.

Grace was particularly special to my father. She was always feisty and he had a soft spot for her. In fact, Grace was so special to my father that her 7th birthday became my father's Heavenly birthday. For years I grieved and dreaded the day until I began to see things differently. He would want us to celebrate, not be sad. Celebrating on that day is not an easy thing to write about because I was so fond of and close to my dad. With all his quirks and eccentricity, he was matchless. My father was also my friend and losing him was agonizing. Yet, death isn't the end, and Mary of Bethany understood that. Though weeping endure for a night, joy comes in the morning. (Psalms 30:5) And death is a tool in our Redeemer's hands.

> "Leave her alone. It was **meant** that she should save this perfume for the day of my burial." John 12: 7 (NLT)

Mary understood and believed something even the disciples couldn't grasp. She had faith that the One who raised her brother from the grave could not possibly stay in the grave. He was too powerful. And by sitting at his feet, she understood that he would be raised from the dead. Notice that Mary was not recorded at the cross. She had such insight. She understood the secrets from sitting at His feet. Attentive Mary who sat at His feet knew there wasn't much time left. The disciples weren't that intuitive. Mary understood the secret of His death and resurrection. She had experience with resurrections after her brother was raised from death. She was preparing for Jesus's burial.

God's Purpose

"Lord if you had been here, my brother would not have died." Martha believed that if Jesus had been in Bethany, Lazarus would have had a chance to live. However, Martha needed to understand that Jesus was not limited by space, distance or time. He did not have to be at Lazarus's bedside to heal him. Jesus could have spoken the word when he first heard Lazarus was sick, and he would be healed.

Jesus took the interlude between the time he got to Mary and Martha's house before raising Lazarus from the dead to address a critical need. You see, with Jesus the focus was not on the miracle. We read this passage but miss the main purpose of the passage. It's not about Lazarus. It's about Jesus's power over death.

Jesus allowed everything to play out so He could orchestrate the right circumstances to set His revelation. That's why even though the Bible says, "Jesus loved Martha, Mary and Lazarus, **so when** he heard that he was sick he **stayed two more days** in the place he was." (John 11:5-6) Lazarus, Martha and Mary of Bethany were dear friends of Jesus. In fact, Jesus's fondness for Lazarus inspired the shortest verse in the bible, "Jesus wept." (John 11:35) But Jesus had a purpose for his delay. **Has Jesus ever put you on hold?**

I imagine when the information was given to Jesus about Lazarus, they told him Lazarus was in critical condition. He was at the point of death. What sickness Lazarus had is not mentioned, but the concern of his sisters shows it was serious enough to send for the Lord.

Jesus still did not come. Even though Jesus knew how sick Lazarus was, He did not come. After Jesus knew Lazarus was dead, he did not go to the funeral. He did not go to the burial.

God's Ways are Different

Jesus was only roughly two miles from Bethany. He could have walked there in about thirty minutes. However, He chose to wait. This was hard for the sisters to understand. Yet, in seeing Him raise Lazarus from the dead, Mary was able to understand that Jesus had a higher purpose in what He had allowed her to endure. So it is with us. We are not always able to understand what God is doing in our lives until His purpose is fully revealed.

I recall a story I heard years ago about a young successful preacher who became rich. He was engaged to a wealthy lady. When she became sick and died, it broke his heart. He lay on the floor for hours each day for two or three months weeping and deeply distraught. Later, he went to India as a missionary and gave away his great wealth to those people. For forty years living in a small room, he served God and those around him. He became known in India as a devoted saint. God sometimes redirects our plans and our affections that we may pour out our prayers, love, and tears on the feet of Jesus that we may gain greater understanding for it.

Death is a Tool

God does not view death the same way we do. We

mourn and grieve as if we have no hope. But God views death as an entry point to eternity. Death is not an end, but overly simplified, it is ingress to the endless. Though I miss my loved ones who have gone before me, I cannot live despondent and despairing. Instead, I must do my part to share the hope I have with all I meet, so we can all look forward to the infinite together.

Not completely grasping all that lie ahead eternally, I trust absolutely that my loving Creator, who formed me with all my delights and displeasures, has my best interests at heart. God has something so captivatingly extraordinary in store for those of us who believe.

I am the Resurrection and the Life

After Jesus told Martha, "Your brother shall rise again," she demonstrated her faith and understanding of the believer's resurrection to come by saying, "I know my brother will rise again at the resurrection in the last day." Jesus seized the moment to introduce a crucial revelation about himself to Martha.

Martha understood that God would raise people from the dead at the resurrection. But Martha needed to understand who Jesus really was. He asked her, "You believe in the resurrection?" Then He answered, "I am the resurrection!"

Jesus identified himself as God by making this statement. "I AM," in short means, the self-existent one. When Jesus said, "I am the resurrection and the life," He was claiming to be the source of both. There is no resurrection apart from Jesus, and there is no eternal life apart from Jesus Christ.

First Jesus said, "I am the resurrection"—this is the direct answer to Martha's profession. Second, Jesus said, "I am the life". He did not simply say that He gives resurrection and life, but that He IS resurrection and life. In Him the life of the age to come, after the resurrection, is already present and available.

Jesus is the resurrection in the sense that whoever believes in Him, although dying physically, will live spiritually. Jesus is the life in the sense that whoever lives spiritually—whoever has received the gift of life through belief in Jesus—will never die a spiritual death. The one who believes, even though he dies physically, will live spiritually.

In the book of Genesis, we see that when God created man, he breathed spirit, (life) into the physical body of Adam, who became a living soul. Because God breathed a part of His eternal breath into our beings, that spirit can never cease.

Paul said in 2 Corinthians 5, " For we know that if our earthly house, this tent, is destroyed, we have a building from God, not made with hands, eternal in the heavens."

We do not die eternally because John 3:16 says, "For God so love the world that he gave his only begotten son that whosoever believe in him **will not perish** but have eternal life."

The day our heart responds to the call of God to believe that Jesus is the way of salvation and place our faith in what the Bible says about Jesus, we ensure eternity. At physical death, we enter into the presence of the Lord in Spirit and await that bodily *resurrection Martha was talking about*.

Greater Understanding

If Lazarus had not died, Mary would not have known that Jesus could raise him from the dead. Yet, after Lazarus died, she understood firsthand all about the great power of the Lord Jesus. Again, when we go through trials, we might question the Lord's wisdom in allowing us to endure some of the things we face. But when He comes through for us, then we know personally that He has all power in heaven and in earth! When we learn this truth, it increases our faith and helps us to trust more fully in Him and His power.

Martha, Mary and Lazarus were experts in divine relationship. In fact, Jesus was a frequent guest in their home. He loved Mary, Martha and Lazarus, and they loved Him; and Mary sat at His feet, listening to His teaching. From this, she would come to know of His death, His burial, and His resurrection. From this would the Holy Spirit put into her heart to anoint Him for burial.

Mary was a spiritually sensitive woman. She knew even better than her older sister what Jesus needed most. Jesus was physically and mentally worn with the unrelenting demands of the multitudes. Wherever He walked, He was pushed and pressed by curious crowds. He was especially harassed by pointed challenges to His truth and mission. He was human. He knew weariness of body and spirit, and He needed understanding and fellowship. This Mary gave Him, and He commended her and blessed her for it.

Mary's Anointing Fulfills the Prophesy of the Spikenard

By being spiritually sensitive, Mary fulfilled prophesy. Interestingly enough, I found a parallel verse that seems to refer to Mary's devotion in *Song of Solomon*. Mary's perfume was spikenard. Solomon foretold a thousand years earlier of this significant event. Song of Solomon 1:12 says, "While the king [sitteth] at his table, my spikenard sendeth forth the smell thereof."

This verse mentions the smell, which John also records, while the king reclines at the table. This parallel shows Mary of Bethany as a representation of the Church (the bride), as Song of Solomon is an allegory between the Bridegroom and His Bride. Woman characters throughout scripture often point to greater spiritual parallels. In Song of Solomon, the bridegroom is inviting her to come and join Him at the marriage supper feast. The bride's fragrance emanates from her spirit in worship and adoration for the King's provision. This is a Heavenly fragrance we all should possess. And Mary, because she sat at His feet, developed a sensitive spirit to understand such things.

Mary Understood Secrets

From her first encounter with Christ, Mary seems to have pursued one thing above all – the deepest possible relationship with Him. She soaked up His teaching, took His promises to heart, listened for every change of intonation that would yield more clues about Him. Love gave her insights that others missed. She could have discerned that Jesus would enter Jerusalem not to lasting acclaim but to death and dishonor. For a time, the light itself would appear to be stifled by the darkness. While everyone else was busy celebrating Jesus's triumph in raising Lazarus at the feast, Mary stood quietly beside him, sharing his grief in what was to come.

She knew Jesus held the keys to eternity, so she acted as such. Mary did not give much thought or take into account the world's system. She sought to honor and obey God in the purest, most extravagant way she could. Mary embodied the verse that says, "[2] Don't copy the behavior and customs of this world, but let God transform you into a new person by changing the way you think. Then you will learn to know God's will for you, which is good and pleasing and perfect." (Romans 12:2) She lived in the earthly world but she was not of it.

In the midst of all this symbolism and foreshadowing, Jesus saw something else at work. He interpreted Mary's act of worship as preparation for His burial. When the disciples rebuke her for what they deemed a waste of money, Jesus responded by saying, "Let her alone; why do you trouble her? She has performed a good service for me. For you always have the poor with you, and you can show kindness to them whenever you wish; but you will not always have me. She has done what she could; she has anointed my body beforehand for its burial."

Jesus had been speaking of His impending death for a while, but the twelve could not understand or grasp His message. When Jesus told Peter, "the Messiah must be rejected, suffer, and die; then he will be raised," (Luke 9:22), Peter responded with such an impassioned protest that Jesus rebuked him with "get behind me Satan!" (Matthew 16:23). In another instance, Jesus spoke ominously of His death, and the disciples responded by debating who will be the greatest in the coming kingdom. Then, James and John missed the point entirely by responding to Jesus' prediction with requests to sit at his right and left hand. Clearly, the disciples struggled to perceive a kingdom that would begin not with the death of their enemies, but with the death of their Master. I suspect this is why they complained about the "waste" of money exhibited by the anointing. The disciples imagined that their ministry with Jesus would continue for months and years to come. You can sense the sadness in Jesus's words when He reminds them, yet again, that He will not always be with them, that He is preparing for the most difficult days of his life.

So Mary of Bethany becomes the first of Christ's followers to acknowledge His looming death. For this, Jesus praises her in unparalleled terms. *"Truly I tell you, wherever the good news is proclaimed in the whole world, what she has done will be told in remembrance of her."* Jesus wanted us to remember her sensitivity and her worship, but have we forgotten?

Seek a Hearing Heart. Godly Wisdom

Mary showed evidence of knowing more of His power and mission than even His disciples. She had heard Him speak of His death, and she knew that some things were worth dying for. In her eyes, whatever He did was right. Mary, passionate and pensive, is perhaps the most spiritually sensitive woman in the Bible.

Mary had often heard Jesus speak of His coming death and burial, and her alabaster jar of precious ointment had been treasured up for the anointing of His body. *She heard His words*. Words of comfort, words of love, sweetness, and tenderness. She sat at His feet and drank in the deep meaning of His words and gazed into the depths of His Spirit.

The alabaster jar contained a pound of spikenard ointment. It was Mary's treasure chest, a hope chest, if you will. The day was coming for it to be opened. This was not a whim, not a sudden impulse. Surely the emotion of the moment had been building within her. Then she brought it out and used it to dedicate the Lamb of God to the sacrifice He was about to make. "Against the day of my burying hath she kept this," and Jesus appreciated the fragrance of that ointment while He was alive.

Mary's heart anticipated what lay deepest in His, even before it found expression in words. She not only knew that He would die, but she apprehended the infinite preciousness and value of that death. And how more fitting could she have expressed this than by anointing His body "to the burying" (Mark 14:8)! Mary mourned His death and grieved for what He had to endure. Like watching a loved one being diagnosed with a terminal disease, she did what she could.

The Father ordered that His beloved Son should be "anointed" here in this home at Bethany in the presence of Lazarus, whom Christ had raised from the dead: it attested to the power of His Own resurrection!

Consequently, Mary's anointing of the Lord, was a gesture of tremendous significance. Just before the cross, Jesus was being sealed as our King, Priest, and Sacrifice.

Independent Blessing

Jesus gave Mary a memorable reputation. He said, "I tell you the truth, wherever the Good News is preached throughout the world, this woman's deed will be remembered and discussed." (Mark 14:8 NLT) It is more than two thousand years since this incident, and Mary is still remembered for her worship. God tells us that the memory of the just shall live forever. Mary's love and unselfish goodness have been immortalized.

A special blessing is reserved for those who simply listen and hear what God is speaking from His word. Listen to the prophet Isaiah, "Hear and your soul shall live." How simple. Cease your useless struggling; hush the noise of your will and heart; get quiet; listen to Jesus –let only His words whisper into your ears, down into your heart, and it will heal. Sit at His feet, and like Mary, drink deeply from the depths of meaning in His words.

Mary had an independent blessing, Jesus said, "Which shall not be taken from her" (Luke 10:42). Thank God for such a blessing. Christ has a blessing for each of us that shall never be taken from us *without our consent*. God wants to give each of us a blessing that will transform our lives. Do you know gifts and talents are lying hidden away in our souls, which will never be discovered until the Holy Spirit stirs them? When we allow Him to direct us, our lives, words, and actions will bless people. I pray the Holy Spirit reveals these things to our hearts and gives each of us a Mary-like experience, which shall not be taken away from us.

Mary knew love. She knew it, not as a fact, but as a person. She was personally acquainted with God's love in human form. She was already living the teaching of the Master. His followers should love in the same way that the Father loved Him. In so doing, they would abide in His love.

Mary lived in love. Love that would not endure merely *to* death, but *through* death. She received it and responded to it. A broken alabaster jar offers proof of that.

Dig Deeper Devotion

What is Jesus's special blessing for you? Are you aware of the gifts and talents that lie dormant in your soul? When we allow Jesus to direct us, our lives, our words, and our actions will begin to bless others. Allow the Holy Spirit to reveal these things to your heart and give you a Mary-like experience which shall not be taken away from you. Think on what these might be.

____
____
____
____
____

Meditate on These Verses

> 2 Corinthians 5:1, "For we know that if our earthly house, this tent, is destroyed, we have a building from God, not made with hands, eternal in the heavens."
>
> Matthew 6:33, "But seek first the kingdom of God and His righteousness and all these things will be added unto you."

Challenge

Mary knew that death was not the end. She knew how to worship through very difficult circumstances. What circumstances can you bring before Jesus to use to worship Him?

____
____
____
____
____
____
____
____

Connect

Write back to God about your life, what you read, or a request on your heart.

____
____
____
____
____
____

Prayer

Jesus, please allow us to see our lives on earth as a fleeting moment compared to eternity. Help us to live our days with eternity in view and honor You and love those you have blessed us with in life. Amen.

Chapter 13: Misunderstood

"When the disciples saw this, ***they were indignant. 'Why this waste?'*** *they asked."* - Matthew 26: 8 NIV

But there were ***some who were indignant among themselves****, and said, "Why was this fragrant oil wasted?* [5] *For it might have been sold for more than three hundred denarii and given to the poor."* ***And they criticized her sharply****.* - Mark 14:4-5 NKJV

My mother does things differently. She doesn't understand why others don't do things her way. Mom does first and asks later. She is blacklisted at some airports for her antics and does not understand why they don't like her. Surely, it has nothing to do with the trip she took years ago. My parents were moving cross-country, and she took advantage of the frequent trips up north to tie up loose ends by filling her luggage and pushing the weight limits of the bags. It made total frugal sense to her to move bit-by-bit since she had so much family up north and still made frequent visits. On this trip she decided to pack up the garage and crammed a duffle bag full of screwdrivers, hammers, box cutters and other tools. She shoved the heavy bag into her checked luggage and was hardly able to close it. Needless to say, when they weighed her bag, it was too heavy. She went into damage control mode and quickly unzipped the suitcase and removed some things and heaved them into her carry-ons.

After she removed her shoes and neatly placed her bag on the conveyer, she was startled to find the alarms around her sounding and a team of people rushing toward her. Thinking there was a terrorist around, she moved aside only to be apprehended and brought into an interrogation room. My youngest sister who was traveling with her was shocked by the happenings and ~~screamed at~~ urged her to stop talking in her thick Middle Eastern accent (for the love of all things holy!) and vowed never to travel with her again. The Arabic sermon tapes, bottles of perfume and Middle Eastern name added to the TSA's suspicion. As Middle Eastern Christians we are the minority of the minority, but try explaining that to the TSA agents with a handbag full of box cutters and tools. She was able to clarify and reluctantly forfeit her bag after many hours.

Rules don't apply to my mother. Rules didn't apply to Mary of Bethany, either. Or so it seemed.

Mary was misunderstood. She didn't follow the rules and was criticized for it. Are you misunderstood in your worship? He created you uniquely, and distinctive will be your worship.

A Lavish Display of Love

Among all the Bible examples, a few people stand head and shoulders above others when it comes to their devotions and worship to the Lord: King David, Daniel and Mary of Bethany.

Worshiping the Lord is more than just singing a few songs. True worship comes from the heart of the believer of Jesus Christ. Mary of Bethany illustrated sincere worship.

John 4:23 tells us that, "… the hour is coming, and now is, when the true worshipers will worship the Father in spirit and truth; for the Father is seeking such to worship Him." True worship to our Lord Jesus requires our lives, our devotions, even the money we are allowed to steward.

The Background Story

Mark 14:1-2, "After two days it was the Passover and the Feast of Unleavened Bread. And the chief priests and the scribes sought how they might take Him by trickery and put Him to death. [2] But they said, "Not during the feast, lest there be an uproar of the people."

The event described above took place six days before Passover, which would put it on the Friday before the Triumphal Entry – Jesus final entry into Jerusalem. By placing the story of Mary preparing Jesus for burial between the accounts of the plot to arrest Jesus, Mark contrasted the treachery of Judas and the religious leaders with the love and loyalty of Mary. The ugliness of their sins makes the beauty of her sacrifice even more meaningful.

Ancient Israel celebrated Passover as a great celebration of independence from Egypt. It was a time to celebrate God's deliverance from the slavery, of singing traditional Jewish songs and more. Every male Jew who lived within fifteen miles of Jerusalem traveled to Jerusalem for Passover, but many more came from great distances. Many families who heard and saw Jesus in the region of Galilee were there, with great respect and expectation for Jesus.

At this particular Passover, however, the mood inside the temple was not so festive. Instead of celebrating, a few influential religious leaders were planning an execution of Jesus, just because He was a credible threat to their power and position.
As the chief priests and scribes conspired to murder an innocent man, they showed that they did not fear God. They did, however, fear the people. These leaders were more concerned about their own political and social positions than doing what was right in the sight of God.

A Lavish Love

Mark 14:3, "And being in Bethany at the house of Simon the leper, as He sat at the table, a woman came having an alabaster flask of very costly oil of spikenard. Then she broke the flask and poured it on His head."

Friend and foe were moving toward the cross, but by different routes. Mary of Bethany came in the way of light and love. Judas was moved by greed and dark motives. And, by the way, it is John who tells us that this woman was Mary, the sister of Martha and Lazarus in John 12:3.

This isn't the same event as when a sinful woman brought the alabaster flask of ointment, broke it and anointed Jesus' feet in Luke 7. That occasion was precious, but it was different because the woman was overwhelmed with her own sense of sinfulness and adoration to the Lord who forgave her sins. Mary seems focused on Jesus alone, not even on her own forgiven sin. Loving Jesus for all He has done for us is easy. But it can be greater still to love Him simply for who He is in all His wonder and majesty.

Mary gave lavishly and lovingly. She didn't dispense a few drops of the fragrant oil on His head. She easily could have, and no one would blame her for saving the rest for herself. But she broke the flask and didn't hold anything back.

Mary was not ashamed to openly display her love for Christ. When we show our genuine love and worship toward our Savior Jesus, it brings mixed reactions from those who are around us.

When we offer our gifts of devotion to Jesus in a way that honors him, when we break ourselves open and pour ourselves out, we are always vulnerable to critique. Others might not understand. Others might judge us and our actions. Others will wish we devoted our time, money and energies in different ways.

In the same way that our corporate acts of devotion to Jesus will be misunderstood and criticized, so will our individual acts of devotion to Jesus. In the face of these criticisms, and misunderstandings, we can find great comfort in knowing that Jesus defends us. Jesus sees and understands. Jesus receives and remembers.

Criticized

Mark 14:4-5, "But there were some who were indignant among themselves, and said, 'Why was this fragrant oil wasted? [5] For it might have been sold for more than three hundred denarii and given to the poor.' And they criticized her sharply."

Yes, it was an expensive offering that Mary gave to the Lord. The Gospel of John tells us that Judas led the grumbles among the disciples. The pious suggestion that the proceeds be used for charitable purposes covered up the real reason. Judas wanted it for his own selfish ends.

Judas criticized Mary for "wasting money," but he wasted his entire life. So, Judas, materialistic thief that he was, led others to complain.

While the odor of the spikenard was sweet to many, it smelled of waste to others. The disciples argued over what they thought to have been wasted. They counted the creation of greater value than its Creator, quibbling over the finite when the Infinite stood before them.

Worshiping the creation rather than the Creator: that's a mistake. Letting a person other than Jesus be our chief concern, that's an inaccuracy. Saying that extreme giving to honor Jesus is wasted, that's a delusion.

Why do some people feel that to exalt themselves requires putting someone else down? Judas objects to the extreme extravagance of Mary's gesture. Completely uncommon worship is often misunderstood.

As she broke the alabaster flask and poured the ointment upon Jesus, Mary illustrated to us about true worship that:

1) True worship comes from brokenness.

When finally we're at our wits' end and broken, we can humble ourselves before the Lord and truly worship Him. Mary wanted to be around Jesus despite culture and the cost to her reputation. Psalms 34:18, "The Lord is near to those who have a broken heart, and saves such as have a contrite spirit."

2) True worship is often costly.

It cost Mary a lot. What does our worship cost us? Our image, our pride? "There's no way I'm going to sing those songs. I'm too cool for that," or "I don't care if Scripture declares lifting hands is a sign of submission and adoration, but I'll never lift mine. People might think I'm weird."

If that's the case, whom do you worship? If God is the focus of your worship, it really doesn't matter what others think or even what you think.

3) True worship is often misunderstood.

People like Judas will say, "Quit trying to be so holy. Do something more practical." They will scrutinize your sincere motive of worship. Let them. God loves your worship. However, if you are causing a commotion and bringing attention to yourself instead of God, that is not worshiping the Lord.

4) True worship is always beneficial.

After Mary anointed her Lord Jesus, people could smell the fragrance all over the house. That's what worship does. When we're worshiping the Lord, we get to take on the fragrance of the Lord.

A Great Defense

Mark 14:6-8, "But Jesus said, "Let her alone. Why do you trouble her? She has done a good work for Me. [7] For you have the poor with you always, and whenever you wish you may do them good; but Me you do not have always. [8] She has done what she could. She has come beforehand to anoint My body for burial."

Notice that Mary didn't defend herself from the grumblers for what she had done. She simply did what she felt led to do by the Spirit of God. In turn, Jesus Himself defended her.

Please remember this: If you did what God told you to do according to His way, you don't have to defend yourself. You have the best advocate in the universe in your corner.

No matter what others say about our worship and service, the most important thing is that we please the Lord. The fact that others misunderstand and criticize us should not keep us from showing our love to Christ. Our concern should be His approval alone.

By the way, how in the world did Mary know to anoint Jesus for His burial? Because each of the times we see Mary of Bethany in the Bible, she is at the feet of Christ. Remember, Mary listened and believed the teaching of Jesus while the disciples didn't. When He said that He would be delivered into the hands of wicked men and mocked, scourged, and crucified, she believed it.

Jesus told the disciples to leave her alone and stop criticizing her. Jesus rebuked them and said she had done a good work, for He knew His life would soon be broken, just like the alabaster jar filled with the costly scent. Not a drop of her extravagant act of worship was wasted in His eyes.

Commemoration

Mark 14:9, "Assuredly, I say to you, wherever this gospel is preached in the whole world, what this woman has done will also be told as a memorial to her."

If it were not for Mary, her village of Bethany would have been forgotten. The account of her deed was a blessing to the church and, because of the records in three of the Gospels, Mary's worship has been a blessing to the whole world – and still is!

The disciples longed for fame and influence, but this woman is the one who found an enduring memorial. She discovered it not by longing for a position, but simply by loving Jesus and worshiping Him irrationally.

Misjudged

I recall when my oldest daughter was about nine years old. She and I have an interesting connection mostly because of the similarities that irritate us about ourselves that are evident and often glaringly obvious when they are staring you in the face every day. Oftentimes, there is no escaping how frustratingly similar we can be. Opinionated, strong-willed first-borns we butt heads on everything. Yet, it was in a worship service that I remember God prodding my heart about this wild worshipping girl trying to make a place for herself in this world. I looked over as the music and voices crescendoed around us and I saw my "mini-me" arms raised in abandon belting out louder than those around us the words to her own song. My instinct was to shush her and put her in her place so she could stop drawing so many eyes. But I felt God whisper to my heart, "Let her be, I love her unrestrained worship." Before I could protest the voice, it was followed quickly by, "And stop rejecting in her what you don't like about yourself." Immediately the flood gate of tears had been loosed and I couldn't stop the emotion from overwhelming me. Had I been rejecting her all this time because of the things I hated about myself? Some part of me was, and still God was at work in this imperfect heart and choosing to love me. Lily has taught me more about myself and has grown me as a woman and a mom. I think it a bit unfair that first-borns tend to be the Guiney pigs of their immature parents and I continue to repent and do better. But truly this beautiful gift of a child has taught me more about God's grace than any other experience in life and I am forever grateful.

We must never disregard or devalue anyone else's acts of service. Sadly, we see Christians do this all the time. Some don't care for the style of praise songs, or the sermon's length or the tears of a broken person being too dramatic. Let's not be too distracted complaining about others to worship our Lord and Savior. If we find ourselves complaining about someone else's act of worship, maybe we should think twice. But, be advised, extravagant worship of Jesus is never a mistake.

What is Jesus worth to you? To Mary, He was worth everything she had. To Judas He was worth thirty pieces of silver.

Giving Ourselves in Worship

Romans 12:1, "I beseech you therefore, brethren, by the mercies of God, that ye present your bodies a living sacrifice, holy, acceptable unto God, which is your reasonable service."

The next step in worship is the offering of a surrendered life. It is the place of sacrifice and consecration. When we decide to follow Christ, we must be willing to be regarded as strange, even by those who used to be our close friends. This is also true in worship. We might believe our expression of love for Christ to inspire others to worship. Yet sometimes our worship in sacrificial giving not only has no influence on others, it can also bring us into conflict with other believers.

Worshipers at this level offer themselves as living

sacrifices. We express our love in joyous sacrifice, cheerfully giving all because of our love for the Savior. We pour out of our lives because of our love for the Lord.

Mary's Worship of Giving

(John 12:1-8) Christ was everything to Mary and the ointment gave her an opportunity to express her love for the Lord. Her worship was done openly in the presence of the disciples. In one moment, she poured the costly ointment on the Lord and nothing could be saved of the fragrance that immediately filled the room. The disciples did not appreciate Mary's act of worship; they were aware only of the money that had been wasted. Mary worshiped at the level of giving *all* out of love for the Lord Jesus Christ.

Mary in Bethany adored in total surrender. Those who have no desire to worship will not understand worshipers who joyously pour out their lives in worship. Many Christians had to face severe opposition from other believers when they turned their backs on success and prosperity to serve Christ. The world did not become angry at Mary's expression of worship; it was the disciples who became angry at her act. When our brothers and sisters in Christ misunderstand our actions, we must respond with tenderness and love. If we lose our joy by coming into conflict with others, then we will go down from the place of worship. The joyfulness of a surrendered life will be lost unless we learn to abide in the love of the Lord Jesus.

This place of worship can inspire people of like

mind, but it often has little effect on others. Only those who have surrendered their lives as a living sacrifice are able to reach this level of worship.

The poor widow was able to worship with sacrificial giving even though she had only two mites, the smallest coin in Bible days. Her offering was special because she had nothing left. She had given all she had, and in her poverty, she could reach to this height in worship. *"...but she of her want did cast in all that she had, even all her living."* (Mark 12:44) The poor widow worshiped God in a wonderful way, but it had little effect upon anyone else. If the Lord had not brought it to His disciples' attention, nobody ever would have known what she did. Worship at this level is often very personal, and even though it is a wonderful place of worship, its significance can pass without being noticed by others. But that is not the point of that level of worship anyway.

When we give our hearts and lives entirely to the Lord, we are giving back to Him only that which He has given us. We are stewards of our lives, and we must learn to worship in sacrificial giving. Whatever we give to the Lord must be given with joy. (2 Corinthians 9:7) The joyous giving of our lives to the Lord as an act of worship is very personal and can be misinterpreted by others. Mary's selfless act of worship in Bethany was entirely motivated by her love for the Lord, yet the disciples did not see it that way. The Lord commended her for it. Worshipers must learn to be unaffected by the reaction of others. This height of worship is also the place of brokenness. When we worship at this level, we must come with tender hearts that are broken before the Lord to avoid being drawn into contention with others.

Weird Worship Teaches Us

Mary's worship could have been considered weird. Weird worship shows us that there are times when the common sense view fails. On this occasion, the voice of common sense said, "What waste!" and no doubt it was right. But there is a world of difference between the economics of common sense and the economics of love.

Common sense obeys the orders of prudence; but love obeys the dictates of the heart. Common sense has a place in life, but there are times when only love's extravagance can meet love's demands. A gift is never really a gift when we can easily afford it; a gift truly becomes a gift only when there is sacrifice behind it, and when we give far more than we can afford.

Weird worship shows us that certain things must be done when the opportunity arises, or they can never be done at all. We can do some things at any time. Some things that can be done only once, and to miss the opportunity to do them then is to miss the opportunity forever. Often, we are moved by some generous impulse and do not act upon it. The circumstances, the person, the time, and the impulse will never return. For so many of us, the tragedy is that life is the history of lost opportunities to do a lovely thing.

Delayed obedience is really disobedience in disguise.

Dig Deeper Devotion

Where might you be vulnerable to misunderstanding or criticism? Perhaps your own self- criticism will plague you the most. Now, rather than focusing on the voices of the accusers, take some time to listen to Jesus, your defender. What does He say to you?
Would you pour it all out as we worship Him? Don't hold back. Don't worry about what others might think. Give Him all you've got. After all, He gave you His best Jesus Christ.

____

____

____

____

____

Meditate on These Verses

> Romans 12:1, "Therefore I urge you brothers, in view of God's mercy to present your bodies as living sacrifices…"
>
> Psalms 34:18, "The Lord is near to those who have a broken heart, and saves such as have a contrite spirit."

Challenge

How pure, how deep, how lavish is your love for Christ? If it can be bottled, would it be sweet fragrance to our God or would it be a stench to Him because of our unwillingness and selfishness? Our worship and lives should be lavish displays of our love for Jesus, because He alone deserves it all.

How much of yourself do you truly give to the Lord? Is it 10 percent? What if this week you gave 20 percent? What if you decided that you would give 50 percent of yourself next month? Are you using what you have to bring glory and honor to Him, or are you keeping all to yourself? Follow Mary's example. What are you willing to give?

____

____

____

____

____

____

____

____

____

Connect

Write back to God about your life, what you read, or a request on your heart.

____

____

Prayer

Jesus, I feel like my worship can be judged by others and misunderstood. Please help me to worship you in Spirit and in truth, as you want. Help me not to look to others' approval of my worship. Amen.

Chapter 14: Filling in the Margins

"Leave her alone," Jesus replied. "It was ***intended*** *that she should save this perfume for the day of my burial." John 12:7 NIV*

"But Jesus said, 'Let her alone; she has ***kept*** *this for the day of My burial.'" John 12:7 NKJV*

We lived in Florida for a number of years. So naturally I became familiar with most of the beaches. I have a thing for salt water and sand. The rest of my crew, not so much. It's my happy place. It's their sticky sandy torment. I've always had to develop elaborate schemes to get them to humor me and go to the beach. One such scheme was a tiny island called Sanibel. The Internet promised spectacular views and unequaled waters, but the real treasure was on the shores. The island's geographical position provided a cache of seashells, miles and miles of beautiful shells, it was an all-you-can-collect prize all its own. And it was enough of a lure to get my tribe to go.

Sanibel was so famous for its shells; it had a nickname for the posture of its patrons. The "Sanibel stoop" was people hunched over with their bottoms up and their heads-down collecting treasure. And it became our position of choice that vacation. We went home heavily laden with treasures.

Mary of Bethany knew how to collect as well. In the original language, the word "kept" in the verse above means collected, reserved. She collected drop by drop or one denarius at a time, however we look at this precious oil.

Why do we struggle to find time to pray or read our Bibles? Because we are not always good collectors. I know an evangelist who was a father, a doctor by vocation, and an author. When I asked him how he does it all, his answer surprised me. It holds the key to a secret. "I collect the leftovers of time." *Collected the remains* is the same language used in collecting the bread and fish from the miracle of the feeding of the 5,000 (John 6:1-14).

What do you do with your spare time? Do you know how to reserve and to collect little bits here and there? Or are you unconcerned with the few minutes here and there? Time is precious. Fill your gaps with the Word. Surround your life with worship. Don't waste your time. Collect your spare time.

Mary did what she could (Mark 14:8). She had her unique portion and spent it all!

We have each been given a unique portion. We have no reason to compete with anyone else. Our gifts are as unique as our fingerprints. I implore you to collect your spare time and use it well. Wherever the gospel of good news is preached what Mary did will be spoken of.

I have not watched TV in months. Don't read too much into it. I don't have a super spiritual reason. I simply have had my focus elsewhere. When my vision for what I wanted to pursue became clearer, my priorities changed. I began to fill in the margins of my life. I began to use the drops of time to fill my bucket of writing. See, I too have a lot on my plate. But I don't think that those who accomplish more in life get any more hours to do it. They simply know how to collect.

Ministry doesn't always require a platform. Ministry happens in the moments. What moment can you seize for God's glory? Weary mom next door? Lonely lady at church? Depressed co-worker? Whom can you offer to help in your few precious moments in line at the store? Look for your ministry moments and collect the ones on the fringes. Do the "Sanibel stoop" and collect the ones no one seems to care about.

The "I Don't Have Any Extra Time" Cop-out

I've heard it before. "But you don't understand…I don't have any extra time." I'm asking you to evaluate your situation and collect. Just plan a wedding, have a baby, or get a new job and you will quickly find out how much more you can do with your twenty-four hours.

Four Lies About Time

1. ***I just need to buy some time.*** Did you know that with all the money in the world you cannot buy a moment of time? The Bible shares a story about a woman who had spent all the money she had because she was sick and weak with uncontrolled bleeding (Luke 8:40-56). All the money she had could not stop the bleeding, or make her well, or give her badly needed strength to go on. But when she heard about Jesus, her faith began to build. She mustered all of her might to get close enough to Jesus, simply to touch the hem of His garment. You see, she could not buy time, but she touched the Hem of God's garment and was healed. God controls our time; we cannot buy it.

2. ***I think I will make a little time.*** Do you remember the Bible story of the fool who saw how plentiful his crop was and decided to build bigger barns? (Luke 12:16-21) Jesus called him a fool because his life was going to be taken from him that night. If we could make time, I am sure we would, but it is a Him-possibility. That's right, Him! God makes time we cannot.

3. ***I need to make up for LOST time.*** Friend, there is nothing we can do about the time that has already passed. We all have regrets. We have not used our time as wisely as we should. I wish there were something I could do about all the time I have wasted being unproductive. But the only thing we can do is to wisely use the time we have left.

4. ***I don't have time to study the Bible.*** You have time for the things that are most important to you. It is not as much that you don't have time as it is you do not make it a priority. When you don't want to do something, any excuse will do. "If you wait for all green lights, " someone once said, "You'll never get going." How true that is. You have time left. The question is, "What are your top priorities?" That is where you will spend your time.

"So teach us to count our days that we may gain a wise heart" (Psalm 90:12). I like to think about time as something we sow. We do not actually sow time, but we sow something with the time allotted to us.

Can't Do Much

I also learned that Mary couldn't do much, but she did what she could. That's what Jesus said about her in Mark 14:8, "She has done what she could. She has come beforehand to anoint My body for burial."

Mary could not do many things. Mary couldn't keep the Jewish leaders from falsely accusing Jesus. She couldn't keep the soldiers from crucifying Him or the crowds from mocking Him. But she *could* show her love and devotion by sacrificing the most precious thing she possessed. You might be thinking, "*I can't teach, I can't sing, I can't…, I can't...*" Too often we focus on what we can't do instead of what we can. So what if you can't teach? Not everyone is meant to be a teacher. Can you call a few people and check on them? Can you visit someone who is in the hospital? Can you take food to a food pantry? For us to accomplish great things in God's kingdom, we must all work together, doing whatever we have the ability to do.

Do what you can with what you have where you are.

Irrational Worship

Remember Romans 12:1 said, "Therefore I urge you brothers, in view of God's mercy to present your bodies as living sacrifices... (KJV) this is your "reasonable act of worship." NASV footnotes it "your rational service of worship."

We're looking at Mary's unreasonable worship. It was lavish and extravagant. It was extreme. We're beholding unreasonable worship that Jesus approved. Giving Jesus extreme worship doesn't fit worldly thinking, but it always fits Godly devotion.

What does Mary of Bethany's act of extreme worship teach us? Where does that fit in with us? Extreme worship, though it's often misunderstood, it is never a mistake. Mary was misunderstood. All three times we see Mary at the feet of Jesus, she was misunderstood. She poured out dignity and pride and gave it to Jesus.

Doing something extreme out of love and reverence for the Lord is not a mistake. We should be so courageous, as Mary was, to not care what others think of our extremes in properly worshiping the Master.

Where did Mary get the idea that God is somehow pleased with extreme worship? Well, God ordered some extremes in the Old Testament when it came to worship.

The temple Solomon built required 30,000 men to prepare materials for the building. (1 Kings 6). More than 190 tons of gold and 375 tons of silver were collected for the temple work before it even began. It had to be the best Solomon could make. Extravagance was right. God ordered that. Worship would center around that temple.

So how and where do we do this lavish giving to Jesus? Before you think I'm saying we should have huge, elaborate buildings, understand this: that temple and its furnishings were just a foreshadowing of things to come, things of which Jesus is the reality.

God doesn't live in a building. The Holy Spirit now dwells in the hearts of believers. The center of worship has moved. Worship is now direct. The place for extravagant worship has changed. So what you and I should do as acts of extravagant worship should also fit this change.

I don't expect the average person out there to understand fasting, getting up early for devotions, making sacrifices of time or money so that someone, somewhere, will hear about Jesus. Those things might seem pretty extreme, maybe weird, in some peoples' eyes. But I reply, "So what?" Think it through. Extreme acts of worship are often misunderstood, but they're never a mistake.

Do What You Can

Here's another feature of extreme worship. Though it's never enough, it's always accepted by Jesus. Even Jesus said that Mary did what she could. *Mark 14:8, "She has done what she could. She has come beforehand to anoint My body for burial."*

This trait of extreme worship is actually a negative one, but it's truly a beautiful fact. Do you realize that Mary's worship wasn't enough? She understood that very soon Jesus would die for her. What's that worth? Could one year's wages pay for her salvation? She knew it wasn't enough. God caused the plants to grow to provide the oil. God had placed the alabaster in the ground. God gave Mary her locks of hair, and she had the financial means to own that oil and the strength to be there that day because the Lord gave it to her. She couldn't even give anything to Him that He hadn't given to her in the first place!

No matter how extravagant, our worship to Jesus will never come close to what He deserves. No matter how creative we are, nothing 'wows' the Creator. No matter how much of our energy we pour into worship or how long we use our voices, we'll grow tired. But the praise in Heaven never ceases. No matter how much we give what we consider our own, it's already rightfully God's. No matter how extravagant our worship, it will never be enough. Notice, Jesus didn't say that about Mary's extravagance. She already knew it. It was great, but it wasn't *enough*. Still, it was her *best*. And when we give our best, that honors Jesus. Do we do what we can?

Jesus accepted Mary's worship. He didn't stop her. He did not turn her away. She never worried that she was acting inappropriately. There was no indignant look suggesting that what she was doing wasn't good enough. In fact, nowhere do we ever read of Jesus turning away honest, heart-felt worship to Him – and I'll bet He saw some pretty different expressions of it!

Also, realizing it wasn't enough didn't stop Mary.

She still gave her best at the Savior's feet. Whether her best was good enough, it was still what she would give. She understood He deserved her best.

We should be so deliberate, even though our worship might not seem like much to us or to others. It's never enough; it will never adequately honor Him. But He always deserves it and He always accepts it.

Your singing, no matter how finely polished, isn't perfect like God deserves. Still God deserves the best you can give Him. The way you play an instrument now can't approach how well I think you'll be able to play it in Heaven. Still, God is worthy of your very best *right now*. A poor widow lady knew that her two copper coins didn't amount to much in the temple treasury, but her act of worship was her best to God, and Jesus praised her for that.

Right now, our most extreme acts of worship will never measure up to the glory of Heaven, but they'll always be accepted – just like the crayon scribbles made with love by a three-year-old bring joy to a parent's heart.

Broken but Not a Waste

Here's one more lesson about extreme worship: Though it's always irrevocable, it's never a waste.

Mary had an alabaster jar – not Tupperware®. Once the jar was broken open and the oil poured out, the jar could never be recovered. That's OK. God has always used broken things to His glory: broken soil to produce a crop, broken clouds to give rain, broken grain to make bread, and broken hearts to produce changed lives.

Here, a jar was broken in His honor, and God still uses it.

If we worship Jesus with strings attached, we're not practicing extravagant worship. Mary didn't say, "I'll wait and see if this is worth it." She didn't pour a little on Jesus and wait to see what would happen. She emptied it all out for Him. That's extreme worship, not a waste!

Many times during my pregnancies, I was unable to keep food down sometimes. When my husband would take me out to a nice restaurant, I'd be starving from being unable to eat. I would eat a nice meal. We paid a nice meal price. We'd leave. I'd get physically sick and lose it. The meal came with no guarantees. We were out the money. It couldn't be recovered. But taking a hormonal, discouraged, hungry, expectant mother out to encourage her and show her that you love her isn't a waste. It was always appreciated.

We should be so generous. We should learn to think that nothing we give over to Jesus for His glory has gone to waste – even extreme acts of worship. They are always irrevocable. You can't put worship back into the bottle, but it's never a waste.

No Risk Offer

There's no risk that if you accept Jesus, He will reject you. There's no risk that it would be a mistake to accept Him, that it would be a waste of your life to give it back to Him.

Maybe giving Jesus control of your life sounds pretty extreme to you. If that's the case, join a group of rebels!

Jesus went to extreme measures to buy us back for Himself. He deserves our very best in return.

Dig Deeper Devotion

Where might you collect the wasted time in your life? Can you collect the moments and create a valuable worship experience out of it? Begin to focus on what you CAN do rather than what you can't.

____

____

____

____

____

____

____

____

____

____

____

____

Meditate on These Verses

> Psalm 90:12, "So teach us to count our days that we may gain a wise heart."
>
> Mark 14:8, "She has done what she could. She has come beforehand to anoint My body for burial."

Challenge

How much time is wasted on menial things? Beginning today, start collecting the time you do have and dedicate it to God. If you draw near to Him, He will draw near to you and you will begin to see His mighty hand in your life.

____

____

____

____

____

Connect

Write back to God about your life, what you read, or a request on your heart.

____

____

____

____

Prayer

Jesus, please help my worship and life to be a lavish display of love to you. I believe that you died for my sins, and you alone deserve my heart and my life. Help me to honor you with my days. Wash me with your blood, and forgive me for my sins. I surrender my life to you today and desire to give you control. Amen.

Conclusion

The short story of Mary of Bethany and the few passages that introduce her tell us a great deal about the faith of a woman. She was presumably a young woman in a paternalistic society, but she broke convention and worshipped Jesus in an uncommon way with authentic passion and fierce faith. Let's review her story.

- No matter the name you've been given, or the self-imposed label you put on yourself, today you can change how you see yourself. **Our past does not dictate our future.**

- Seek the ONE thing. **Sit at Jesus' feet and linger, bask and soak in His love for you.** He woos us and invites us deeper into relationship with Him. Accept the offer and draw closer.

- Mary of Bethany teaches us that **nothing is too precious for our Savior**. What occupies your thoughts most? That's your most precious love, thought, etc.? Are you ready for an uneven extravagant exchange? Give Him your precious and discover what He has been desiring to lavish on you in exchange.

- Even when things don't seem to work in your favor, God's view of your life is perfect and complete. **Allow Him to unfold His best plans in your life.**

- Dive deeper into His love. Remember that smitten people do strange things and **allow yourself to fall more in love with your Creator.**

- When Mary broke the jar, she was signaling to us significance in her actions. She whispered without a word, "I could never use what is meant to bring you glory for any other purpose. Are we broken vessels? **Let His light shine through your brokenness.**

- Anointing Jesus's head with oil affirmed Jesus as King. **Is Jesus the King of your life?**

- Anointing His feet signified making Jesus Lord. The difference between a King and Lord is the King has authority while your Lord indicates relationship. Lords guide. **Let Him lead as Lord in your life.**

- When Mary undid her hair and placed it under His feet, she placed her glory under her Master's feet. How hard do you hold on to your pride? **Can you place your pride under His feet?**

- Reading of when the house was filled with the fragrance of the extravagant gift reminds us that when we are with Jesus we carry His scent. What do you smell like? You pick up the aroma of those you are around most. **Carry the scent of Jesus, others are seeking it.**

- Mary didn't fight for her rights. Sometimes we need to look at things differently in order to have a different outcome in life. **Jesus always looks at the heart and motivations of a person not at the outward appearance.** Begin to look at people with eyes of compassion, and see them differently.

- Mary understood the secret of His death and resurrection because she listened to Him and had experience with resurrection of Lazarus. She knew that Jesus held the keys to eternity, so she acted that way. **Mary didn't give much thought to the world's system...do we?**

- Mary was misunderstood. Are you willing to be misunderstood in your devotion to your Savior?

He created you uniquely, and distinctive will be your worship. Let Him show you.

- Mary knew how to collect. She saved for her extravagant offering. Do you know how to collect? **Time, money, and resources are all collectable items available to offer up if we learn how.**

- **His grace is exceedingly above all our thoughts or imaginations and far greater than we can earn in a thousand lifetimes.** Taste and see His goodness for yourself.

You have seen how Mary of Bethany stepped out in faith to reach a gracious God, who was her friend. She broke cultural barriers to know Him better and express her devotion to Jesus. How will you follow her example and worship the gracious, extravagant God we know?

ABOUT THE AUTHOR

Diana Asaad has been in Christian ministry for more than twenty years. An international speaker and intensive, faith-based counselor & coach, her influence crosses cultures by bridging the gap that often divides. She offers a compilation of vital information for spiritual growth and discovering passion and purpose in life. She currently resides with her husband and three beautiful daughters in the south and looks forward to writing more books.

BIBLIOGRAPHY OF SCRIPTURES

The New King James Version®. Copyright © 1982 by Thomas Nelson. Used by permission. All rights reserved.

Scripture taken from the New Century Version®. Copyright © 2005 by Thomas Nelson. Used by permission. All rights reserved.

Scripture quotations marked (NIV) are taken from the Holy Bible, New International Version®, NIV®. Copyright © 1973, 1978, 1984, 2011 by Biblica, Inc.™ Used by permission of Zondervan. All rights reserved worldwide. www.zondervan.com The "NIV" and "New International Version" are trademarks registered in the United States Patent and Trademark Office by Biblica, Inc.™

Scripture taken from the Amplified Bible, Copyright © 1954, 1958, 1962, 1964, 1965, 1987 by The Lockman Foundation. Used by permission.

Scripture quotations taken from the New American Standard Bible® (NASB), Copyright © 1960, 1962, 1963, 1968, 1971, 1972, 1973, 1975, 1977, 1995 by The Lockman Foundation Used by permission. www.Lockman.org

The Holy Bible, English Standard Version® (ESV®) Copyright © 2001 by Crossway, a publishing ministry of Good News Publishers. All rights reserved. ESV® Text Edition: 2016

Contemporary English Version® Copyright © 1995 American Bible Society. All rights reserved.

Scripture is taken from GOD'S WORD®, © 1995 God's Word to the Nations. Used by permission of Baker Publishing Group.

Scripture quotations marked HCSB are taken from the Holman Christian Standard Bible®, Used by Permission HCSB ©1999,2000,2002,2003,2009 Holman Bible Publishers. Holman Christian Standard Bible®, Holman CSB®, and HCSB® are federally registered trademarks of Holman Bible Publishers.

Scripture quotations marked (NLT) are taken from the Holy Bible, New Living Translation, copyright © 1996, 2004, 2007 by Tyndale House Foundation. Used by permission of Tyndale House Publishers, Inc., Carol Stream, Illinois 60188. All rights reserved.

Scripture taken from The Message. Copyright Â© 1993, 1994, 1995, 1996, 2000, 2001, 2002. Used by permission of NavPress Publishing Group.